The Rally Handbook

The Rally Handbook

RICHARD HUDSON-EVANS

B. T. BATSFORD LTD London

First published 1972
© Richard Hudson-Evans 1972

ISBN 0 7134 0469 8

Printed in Great Britain by Bristol Typesetting Co Ltd,
Barton Manor, St Philips, Bristol
for the publishers B. T. Batsford Ltd
4 Fitzhardinge Street London W1H 0AH

Contents

Illustrations

All photographs were taken by Dave Grey

Drawings prepared by Derek Barber

1 Introduction

Rallying—the very name conjures up different pictures in people's minds. But, whatever these visions may be, the variations on a theme are sure to spell motorised excitement. Here may be the very last bastion of attainable competition motoring for the enthusiast, particularly he who is not blessed with vast resources of hard cash. It is the participant aspect of the sport that is perhaps its greatest attraction. In rallying at least, the ordinary motorist can still associate his own daily endeavours with this sector of motor sport. Meanwhile the realms of Formula One become further and further removed from his daily commute and a whole era away from that annual holiday motoring trek.

Just as soon as cars shook off the red flag their makers entered the speed race, in the dark ages a very real factor in the inter-make sales race, and ' Competition ' motoring took to the road. It was a logical extension for rival owners of this and that machine to wish to achieve some sort of organisation around their attempts to out-drag their neighbours. And so it was that the out-and-out motorised chariot races rushed inter-city at dare-devil velocities on their way through the history of motor sport only eventually to be legislated against and forced to thrash round the closed roads and banked tracks of Europe. In those far off epics, competition motoring was then surprisingly nearer to present-day classic rallying than many people were to realise. For instance the lot of those early riding-mechanics, maids of all work on the move, were not all that dissimilar to today's co-driver. The trend of the gargantuan motoring extravaganza, in the manner of the London-to-Sydney and the London-to-Mexico, will be for any rally hoping to be really worth its while in the seventies and beyond, to have to rush across the world. The magic of inter-city, just like those golden oldies, as far as the imagination of the general public is concerned, still lives on. Such events are, for mere mortals, larger than life.

First though, the sporting trial was to be the much more leisurely evolution in store for rallying. Perhaps one day, when some other scribe looks at the passage of the sport over the decades, the sporting trial may well prove to have been in years just as important towards the overall picture as the special stage appears to the afficionados of today.

On those sporting trials of yesteryear, motorised gentlemen took their sportscars, or tried to, up hills to time—and were often even timed to make sure they kept to a set average speed between hills. Today of course the old-style sporting trial has virtually disappeared save for the Lands End, the Exeter, and so forth. The purist looks at these classics more as curio than present-day challenge. Even the trial has specialised itself into a few diehards running weird open specials around and about a set of sections, often in the same wood or hilly field. The followers of trials though are every bit as involved and keen on their particular nook of motor sport as any other but the bouncing passengers and 'fiddle' brakes are very far removed from contemporary rallying, even at the humblest end of the club scale.

In the old days, rallying for most people meant sporting trials. Even the Coupe des Alpes was the Alpine Reliability Trial. It was very much a challenge to car and crew to ascend the mountains at all, let alone cover the sections to time.

The Monte was the number one epic in motoring, possibly in the world. In the height of a European winter, it was quite a feat actually reaching Monte Carlo's harbour-front at all— besides avoiding time penalties along the way, remembering the shortage of road clearing equipment in those days before studded tyres and recces.

Perhaps it was the emergence of classic European rallies from the ranks of the most arduous sporting trials that did more than anything else to put rallying on the public map. With a European series at the head of world rallying a whole new back-up pack of British rallies emerged. For instance, it has only been over the last ten years that our own RAC Rally of Great Britain forgot its driving tests on the promenade, and following the Swedish school of special stages, has now forged ahead to become about the most well thought of rally in Europe. Even though the British club rally is very far removed from the European classics on the one hand, or the world shattering Marathons on the other, it is the club rally that is still the backbone to the sport in Britain; and as long as rallying is allowed to continue, this will always be the case. So if you want to get started in rallying in Britain, you do so quite simply by way of the British club rally. In fact so absorbing a pastime is club rallying that for many it becomes more than just a way to internationals, it becomes the be-all and end-all.

A great deal has been written and said about various facets of rallying. I do not profess to be able to encompass all the craft of rallying in these pages by any means but as one who has studied the subject more than most, I do feel qualified to pass on to others many of the tricks of the trade that I have had to learn myself. As a motoring journalist covering rallies, an international driver in factory cars, a preparer of my own vehicles (at my own expense too!), a navigator, and, in the beginning, a marshal, I've naturally stumbled into virtually all the pitfalls that the newcomer will encounter. As a result the only overall motto that I would suggest anybody wishing to benefit in some way from these pages to adopt, if they do go on to actually taking an active part in the sport itself, is to always enjoy it. The day you do not is the day to give it up. But if you do become hooked on it, take pride in taking your sport seriously. I can only hope that you will gain as much satisfaction as I have from what must surely rank as one of the most absorbing action hobbies of all.

Let us now leap right ahead to the point when the novice becomes fully fledged, and, reckoning he knows it all, wants to achieve that happy, yet vulnerable, state of persuading others to pay for his rallying. I say happy because the art of rallying has to be, by the very nature of the equipment needed, expensive, and financial assistance as a reward for successful groundwork is always well received. I say vulnerable because the competition for any assistance is very very intense. There are always likely to be far too many people chasing far too little sponsorship money. So once gained, hanging on to a sponsor is likely to be quite a demanding job in itself. There is always the well-known commercial fact that sponsors can become disenchanted with this year's marketing gimmick, particularly when it has come round to cheque signing time again, and more particularly if the previous year's results and mass media exposure have not been that good.

The next step from sponsorship is the works sponsored car, or should I say works supplied and prepared car, with sponsored crew. Then the ultimate just has to be appointed as the official and paid representative of a motor manufacturer, being actually paid to do one's chosen hobby. The top of the tree, as in so many modern sports, is therefore to be able to turn professional.

It is as well here to say, as I mean to continue, that rallying is very much a team game. Both crew members are of equal importance. You cannot succeed without a good team effort. The team is a three-some: the driver, his number two, and the car. A works drive can be obtained perhaps more easily by being offered the co-driver's seat because the specialised skills involved mean that top-class co-drivers are few and far between.

However, right from the start, it is as well to realise that there are very few opportunities to drive factory cars on events, and even less on a regular basis. Admittedly, there are more factory teams rallying than there are racing but it is just as difficult becoming successful enough to be able to go professional, or more important to be asked to go professional. So stick to having fun and look for a factory seat last of all. Professionals in all sports are notorious for forgetting to enjoy what, to the rank and file of competitors, is a sport. Anyway the trend, even with factory supplied and serviced rally cars, is towards outside sponsors helping to cover some of the costs, even if not all. For instance the time may come when there will be two potential rally drivers lined up in front of a works team manager both being considered for only one slot in the team. It might be the one who has fixed himself up with a sponsor who is most likely to earn the place. I foresee the possibility of sponsored talent becoming more recognised by the factory teams than unsponsored talent. Though whether sponsored teams, and so the sponsor's name, will ever become as important in rallying as in racing is unlikely. I think, because of the greater similarity of the rally car with production example, and so more tangible sales rub-off, that the marque will always be more important than the decal that happens to be predominant on a heavily sponsored entry.

Once you have done sufficient rallying to start being successful on awards lists regularly, then the way is partially open for you to at least consider yourself eligible for joining the sponsor-seeking queues. If you are very lucky, do not mind having to cover your car with advertising stickers. Only go in for what the trade consider major events that are acceptable by them for trade support, then you might be allowed discounts for this and that item of necessary equipment. The gaining of ancillary manufacturers is, of course, the beginnings of sponsored, or at least part-sponsored, rallying and this all comes with becoming established and winning a few things.

The next step is to persuade a large concern, perhaps ideally a local newspaper or garage to take out an entrant's licence from the RAC. You can then carry your own name on events, as well as at least showing them their name in print in the programme before the start, to give them publicity in press reports, even if you do not manage to obtain for them honourable mentions in despatches on the results list afterwards. Far too many rallyists seeking sponsors seem to run around the West End Advertising agencies with an impressive list of achievements. They would do so much better in many cases to concentrate on a local flag-carrying exercise instead. So often, there is far more ' gold in them there hills ' to be found at the bottom of the rallyist's garden. It is a popular fallacy to imagine that only the streets of ' Ad-land ' are paved with gold. In any case, there are far too many concerns in motor sport chasing after the financial support of far too few sponsors. It is all too obvious to say that if any kind of definite guaranteed publicity can be assured by a rally crew, then naturally this will help a great deal to engender positive financial interest from non-publicity media concerns. So the blessing of a newspaper, TV or radio station, even if it is in fact in name only, is a very real step to having a very effective base for a sponsored entry. But you need to have at least some results in the bag before you really have any kind of a product to hawk. The span of being a top professional rally crew member is, like so many professional sports, a short one. If you aim to make the top always remember it's a pleasant well paid interlude with no security—and no long-term future.

But all this is jumping the gun rather. There is much to learn on the path to becoming remotely proficient, let alone successful, at the sport. Much of it will only really come as second nature after a great deal of practice and practice has to be expensive. However, by gleaning just some of the gen from this guide the lessons may, with luck, not prove to be too costly. After all, to shine in any sport, you have to understand the ancient maxim of not running before you can walk. At least in rallying, running too early or blindly jumping in at the deep end is likely to be curbed by the sheer cost of such folly. In any case the principal ingredient, commonsense should over-ride any impatience by the over-enthusiastic novice.

Every sport has its own terminology, the newer sports tending to be surrounded to a greater extent with their own particular jargon. Rallying is no exception, so rather than steer a long course round a particular 'in' term in this book, I have called a spade a spade throughout. Further, at the back, I have added a sort of dictionary of rallying's lingo, the mastering of which I hope will at least give the rank greenhorn sufficient meat on the way to gaining his wings, whilst of course, any reader may find the list of value if they become puzzled by an exact meaning during the marathon in hand—namely this book!

2 The Driver

Although the mechanical and human elements of the sport are of equal importance, I propose, first of all, to consider the various skills that must be mastered by people involved in rallying. As I have already said, it is very much a team game, the members of which may be driver and his navigator (or co-driver, and there is a difference of which more anon), as well as, on larger events, the service crew. Virtually all the tips for each role are relevant to the others. In any case, it is vital that there is an understanding of the other's problems.

In rallying, rather unfairly, it is the driver who makes the headlines. It is the driver who appears on the advertisements endorsing the wearing of safety belts, or extolling the virtues of this and that fog lamp or make of car. Because of the weighted exposure for this member of any rally crew, it is hardly surprising that the public really only think in terms of the driver being the only person who matters on any rally. In the higher echelons of the sport it is undeniable that the speed of the driver is the number one asset of any crew on an International. But, there is more to rally driving than for the hero merely to have the ability of keeping his foot well and truly glued to the floorboards. The qualities required are many and there is much to learn for anyone fancying their chances in the role of rally driver, especially if they want to stay in one piece. Apart from being able to press on occasionally over un-seen roads, the average rally driver has to be more of a master over extremes of motoring conditions than just the stopwatch—he has to be an expert in getting through and therefore an above average driver. Only two qualities have really lingered on from the early cloth capped days: the ability to stay on the road and the necessity to stay out of trouble, both with the law of the land and other road users.

Not that I am saying that the top rally drivers of today, and indeed most of the rally drivers of tomorrow, are going to have to be similar to track drivers who star in some of the controversial apprenticeship single seater formulae, where for ' cage ' read ' transporter ' and for ' wild animal ' read ' slip-streaming racing driver '. But competition in rallying is becoming more intense. With increasingly more competitors becoming better and better at the sport, the overall classification is nowadays often a matter of split seconds—so, prowess at driving extremely quickly in rallying has become just as vital as it is in racing.

But this does not mean that a racing driver, who reckons he is quite good, can immediately climb aboard a rally car to shine on his first event. Even if the event was one where the specially timed roads, closed or open to the public, were known beforehand, there would be too many of them to ever know every twist and turn off by heart. On such events, he would need to depend on pace notes being read to him with great accuracy by his partner or co-driver. He would really have to understand how to drive with these notes, which is not something that can be picked up overnight. The notes have ideally to be compiled by both crew members in recce trips. To be a competent rally driver takes time. It is not an overnight possibility.

A rally driver has to be able to constantly vary his speed, and that of his car. He has to learn to hold back his car to orders from his co-driver. He has to be able to conserve his car. He has to be able to drive smoothly on public roads. He has to finish. Fastest laps mean nothing in rallying. For while a racing driver is soundly asleep at home after a day's racing—or is out on the tiles celebrating a win—a rally driver has to keep going, often all night.

TECHNICAL KNOW-HOW

One of the first things anybody ought to do who wants to drive on rallies at all seriously is to be absolutely familiar with

1 Spectating or marshalling is the best way to observe the masters at work. It takes years of experience to become as good as Roger Clark and Jim Porter, seen here on the 1970 RAC in Kilburn forest.

2 & 3 Undoubtedly the most significant rally car of the 70s will turn out to be the Alpine Renault. Very low overall weight, high engine power, and plenty of ground clearance has combined to produce one of the most formidable Rally cars in Europe.

the working of his steed. The reason is obvious. There are no pits round the next corner. On a rally, a crew has often to fix something awry themselves. Even on the larger events, where vans full of mechanics and friends stream around the route patching up rally cars, the next meeting point may well be several miles further on. Often, without any outside assistance, the crew itself have to effect repairs. With present-day garage costs being what they are, it is most likely that the required mechanical knowledge will be picked up anyway before very long, if it is not there already. For most indeed, on financial grounds, the only way to set a car up for the sport is to do the work oneself. In ninety-nine point nine per cent of rally competitors, it is the driver who works on the car and the co-driver looks after which way the car should be directed on events, as well as coping with all the reams of pre-event paperwork.

The roles ought to be clearly defined at this point. Drivers fix and prepare cars, and therefore are responsible for the car. Co-drivers, number-twos on larger events, or navigators, more usual on British club events where generally navigation is more likely to be of greater importance, look after the office side, and are therefore responsible for time. Naturally, any driver worth his salt will ensure that he knows how to do all the co-driver's jobs, and vice-versa, a co-driver must know how to rally drive too. It therefore generally works best of all, if a driver sticks to the same co-driver, so developing a partnership. The best drivers in rallying tend to have the same co-drivers. Where a racing driver is more of a loner, the rally driver has to be half of a partnership.

Perhaps the only way to become any good at rallying is to go on rallies. Those with a farm, or who know a friendly farmer, may be able to practise round and round fields to their hearts' content, but nothing can really be made artificially the same as a rally route itself. Certainly it might help to compete in Auto-cross events between rallies. There would be no harm done to a driver's driving skill, indeed it would help better than racing to keep the rust at bay. But, success in this, yet another highly specialised section of the sport, would be difficult to come by. Autocross class winners usually tow their cars to events on

B

trailers as a fully equipped road car would be too heavy. The chances of wearing out any rally car before the next rally, if not writing it off, would be very high. Horses for courses, so rally cars in the age of specialisation, should, like their crews, be ideally preserved for the next rally.

The TV Rallycross boom is meaning that assimilated rally conditions are being attempted around a closed circuit, especially for TV viewing. Although rallycross makes a great TV spectacle, indeed being a boom for making motor sport more popular amongst the masses, here again it can never be as much a test for drivers as real rallying. Because it is a regular occurrence around the same type of circuit, preparers have constructed cars specially. Being very close, because that is what the viewers at home enjoy, bodywork tends to become regularly bent and due to progress forcing modifications, apart from the basic overall shape, the cars have ceased in fact to resemble production cars any more. Of course, the skill of being able to drive fast and steady on multi-surface tracks is of like value in rallying, but it is significant that the rallycross specialists do not venture on to pure rallies.

Being kind, it could be said that one man's meat is another man's poison; but, I would be more ruthless in stating categorically that there is no more difficult type of competition driving than rallying. So the top rally drivers could potentially go on to do well in any other forms of motor sport. The fact that they generally tend to stick to rallying is an indication of the sport's magic magnetism, rather than the specialised limitation of its stars' driving prowess. However, many might not realise the relative solitude of the rally driver's lot. It is only glamourous for the few at the top. Rally driving has to take place in wild and remote places, where few people will be watching. Playing to the gallery is futile, as in the main, on mountain tracks and woody wilds, it will be empty. The chances are nobody will see your accident! If therefore the thought of no ambulance and fire marshals being on hand deters you, when you have to drive flat out over a section, do not consider rallying. If the thought of really, but really pushing your own, and in many cases your only, means of transport appals you, then how about tennis instead. Above all, if you find that you are unable to develop into being able to concentrate long enough for a night's hectic motoring, then you are safer back at the pub.

In short, rallying is far too serious a business for the driving to be taken any other way than seriously. You may be able to half-heartedly kick an old leather-covered inflated bladder round a bit of grass, without anything more sobering occurring than a whistle being blown at you occasionally, but a rally car is a lethal weapon to yourself, fellow crew member—and to the property and person of the general public. It is not just your own life that may be at stake when you are at the wheel, nor those who you may unwittingly involve in an error situation, but the future of the sport as a whole. Good public relations are vital for the survival of the sport, which has had quite enough attempts at being outlawed from public roads in the past. A driver should lose time and gain penalties rather than antagonise other road users by endangering their lot with his overtaking.

But enough of generalisations, and on to specifics. Assuming that the outsider is willing to be sufficiently committed to learn, or more important prepared to learn, let me now go on to answering the first specific question—How does one start rallying?

Well, discounting the basic equipment and the special preparation of same and not attempting to go into all the various types of rally that one can have a go on at this stage, as all these things I have covered in detail later on, there is needless to say some basic paperwork that is necessary first.

THE LICENCE BUSINESS

The governing body of motor sport in Great Britain and Eire is the Motor Sport Division of the RAC, who are this area of the world's representatives of the overall body, an organisation called the FIA. After Ministry of Transport legislation governing motor sport on the roads, all rallies in the UK and Eire with more than twelve cars taking part must be run under RAC rules, and with an RAC permit. So, if you want to take part in rallies, and by rallies I do not mean the treasure-hunt frolics of the local sports club, then you have to abide by the system of the motor sporting establishment. Assuming you have a fully fledged MOT car driving licence in force, then your next step is to join one of the hundreds of RAC approved motor clubs. The Motor Sport Division of the RAC's address is 31 Belgrave Square, London, SW1 and you can obtain from them the names and addresses of motor club secretaries in your area. By joining one or more RAC registered motor clubs, you will then carry the second (after the MOT driving licence) piece of admission documentation, namely a current club membership card. At this stage you can compete, through that club, in the mild less than twelve car rallies that are allowed extra the permit necessity from the RAC. This might be an idea, as it will at least give you a clear indication as to whether the sport in its participant form is worth pursuing. As has happened with everything, rallying, when it is really tried in the field beyond the armchair literary ' read all about it in the magazine's ' stage, loses much of its appeal. But it is more than likely I hope that the initial bewilderments of the first twelve car rally, or club organised practice, will spur on the aspiring rallyist into writing straight off to the RAC for stage one of those licences that control in what events people, taking part in rallies, can or cannot compete.

The normal competition licence combines validity for both entering and driving. However, later on, when you are so good that the sponsors are queuing up to enter you on events, they will need an entrant's licence. A special entrant's licence is obtainable from the RAC for such non-driving private individuals. The same goes for registered clubs.

The Rally competition licence is primarily for drivers to take part in rallies, but is also valid for trials, driving tests, or autotests as they now seem to be called, as well as closed to one club (or restricted to a list of clubs) autocross events. If you want to go autocrossing seriously, then you will really need a Speed licence, which is also needed additionally for any rally driver who might like to take part in Rallycross events. The Rally competition licence is a ' by qualification ' affair with three grades: *International* at the top of the tree; next *National*; whilst you start off with *Restricted*. Your first licence under the Rally category, and novice grade of *Restricted*, will be what you will need for all restricted and closed rallies. The qualification for moving on to the *National* grade is that you must have logged up on the special place on the licence three finishes on events, the status of which may be either restricted or closed, with the stipulation of one event at least being of the larger restricted status. This grade of licence of course, once you have qualified for it, also allows you to compete in restricted and closed events, as well as National British ones. National British means that the event is open to all holders of this grade of licence in Great Britain, regardless of which club they belong to. To qualify for the full *International* grade of a Rally licence, which allows a driver to take part in all International rallies, as well as National Open rallies, yet is also all right for all rallies of lower grades too, again is by qualification. In addition to the qualification for the ' National ' grade of finishing in at least three rallies of restricted or closed grade, of which at least one must be restricted, the driver must finish at least one National British rally, or instead two further restricted rallies.

These grades of the licence itself will cost the competitor £1.50 for *Restricted*, £3 *National* and £4 for an *International*. But, it is as well to appreciate that due to the ever increasing cost of running the Motor Sport Division, these fees are likely to go up in price periodically, so they must only be regarded as a guide.

Once the rallyist has his or her full *International* Rally licence, it is obvious that they may want to compete beyond the home internationals in Great Britain and travel abroad. The FIA insist in such cases that all RAC licence holders must obtain prior and specific approval from the Motor Sport Division to enter each foreign event. The fee is 50p per authorisation, plus a further £2 for medical insurance, all very important in the countries of Europe which are not blessed with our National Health Service.

MAKE-UP

The psychological make-up of a rally driver is always a controversial subject. All sorts of ideas have been banded about the place, and even electronic devices have been coupled up to drivers' hearts. One conclusion is certain. To be any good at all in rallying, you have to be a thoroughly proficient driver at speed, who reacts completely automatically to the present situation and is able to think ahead to master a future one.

Having observed at close quarters the world's top rally drivers, many of whom I can now rate amongst my friends, I can refute the sensationalist opinion that many of them are unbalanced nutcases. They are certainly for the most part individualists. The best ones have that very rare combination of qualities, namely considerable tiger and the ability to relax. They all seem to be able to concentrate for abnormally long periods of time, and are all very aware of the need for self-preservation. They are prepared to take risks, but only calculated ones. They have very quick reactions which they have been able to master, so they never over-react. As well as being intelligent, they have commonsense in abundance, and as a rule emotionally uncomplicated and very practical.

Despite being usually very fit people they are still able to really enjoy themselves off duty. Many of them smoke heavily and also think nothing of tucking into ale after a major rally. Indeed, the after rally happenings are often more hair raising than the rallies themselves. But obviously, before an event, however small, it pays even for the amateur, to do some training. Cars sometimes have to be heaved back on their wheels, out of ditches or pushed up icy hills. Physical fitness is important therefore. It is a good test of a competitor's dedication anyway. Late nights before anyone has to stay up all night driving flat out cannot be good for even the most iron constitution.

However, there is no point in taking the keep fit business over seriously. A driver has to be able to relax to be at his best whilst rally driving. Some people in fact drive worse if their normal routine is violently upset. It all depends on the individual. Certainly, too many long night's sleeping are not ideal for being able to adjust to short irregular cat-naps on the move, with somebody else doing some fairly fast driving. This all points to the necessity for a driver to train his system so that he is able to adjust himself to any conditions, to be able to switch on and off, to pull all the stops out, or to trickle along conserving the car.

The old adage of a driver's effort being rated in tenths is not a bad one. So, as a general rule, a racing driver would be at ten tenths all the time. Rally drivers on the other hand would be at eight tenths on the road on a special stage event, and ten tenths on the vital stages whilst on a rally where the road section was an important part of the event too, he would be at nine tenths, reserving his ten tenths effort for any time deciding sections along the route, or special stages if any.

Combating tiredness is often a number one problem in some cases, where otherwise a particular driver has great potential at being able to control his car over the unknown at a competitive speed. Training with shorter nights sleep might help, or there is always the pill if habit plus the sheer excitement of the rally fail to keep the driver awake.

BE PREPARED

As far as drugs are concerned, opinion is very sharply divided. There are two distinct schools of thought as to whether rally drivers ought to conduct their sporting activity under the influence of a drug or stimulant, or not. Well, I have no wish here to condemn taking ' stay awake ' pills, for surely any sane person must realise that it is better for all concerned if a rally driver stays awake at the wheel rather than falling asleep. From bitter experience, it seems to me that most of the very worst rally accidents have occurred, and I have seen them myself, on perfectly straight bits of road. In such cases, the driver has fallen asleep at the helm.

So any purist outcry at sports people having to take drugs to be able to have a maximum advantage attempt at taking part in the sport of rallying must be squashed on the grounds of commonsense. Whether anybody ought to have to take an artificial stimulant to take part in sport anyway is a moral issue which I do not propose to expound in these pages. The thing that really matters is whether a driver is fully aware of the personal effect of a particular stimulant. Some supposed ' wakey-

wakey ' tablets tend to have peculiar side effects. It is as well to make quite sure that the pill you may use does in fact do its job properly, with no unpleasant and unexpected side effects.

Those who lead a really active life, with little chance of relaxing with their normal job during the week are the ones most likely to need something to keep them on the ball through Saturday night. The only cautionary tips for such people to be aware of are the after effects of acute depression as well as the need for a trial run on the pill first to make sure it agrees with their system. Benzedrine tablets work the best, but beware of Amphetamine which can increase courage tendencies in some people and impair judgement of what is or is not possible. It is however absolutely certain, regardless of what they may admit to in public, that the vast majority of top rally drivers do take ' wakey-wakey ' tablets. They will, if ever a census is taken, hotly deny this. But it is so.

The only way such drugs are legally obtained in Great Britain is on prescription through a rallyist's local doctor. Here again, to those who disapprove at this juncture, I would only say this. If you have ever followed a truck driver swerving all over the road, nodding off, or an all-night holiday commuter pottering across the other side of the road in a moonlight coma, you would surely approve of any doctor prescribing such pills in limited quantity. Long distance driving, particularly at night, can have a hypnotic effect on even the fittest person.

EYES OPEN

Incidentally, I have always found Optrex a most useful aid to keeping relatively alert on the longer events. This is marketed in very useful little squeezy applicators, easily stored in a pocket. A quick squirt into the palprebral fissure, or into the corner of the eyes nearest the nose, does wonders at keeping the eye surface fully lubricated. I believe the major reason for drivers dropping off is that their eyelids begin to stick down through lack of tears.

Naturally, the very best way to keep wide awake is to insist upon a window being wide open. But this is often frowned on by the office manager, whose maps and paperwork would then tend to become too active, and in any case might prove to be somewhat of a hazard even to the driver if they were to waft uncontrollably about the inside of the car. Another point to watch about having a window open on one side for too long is that this can set up one of the very worst troubles any rally driver can suffer from, namely sinusitus. Those who have suffered know how very vicious this can be, in fact many top rally drivers have contracted this from time as a result of icy blasts of air hitting one side of their face for long periods, thus setting up an infection. The only cure, despite the many demon concoctions and nasal inhalers on the market, is to have them washed out at a hospital. This is far from pleasant, but is preferable to a drain tube being inserted through the cheek, which quite honestly effectively puts paid to rallying for a long time.

There will always be a row over whether a heater ought to be on or not. I have always been an advocate of a driver's comfort coming first. So, if a driver likes to sit at 200 in the shade, then he should. In fact, personally I have always opted for dressing up according to the prevailing weather conditions, not liking too much use of the heater, as I have always found it does tend to induce driver drowsiness. The best uses for the heater are not keeping the crew warm, but to keep the screen demisted, as well as increasing the radiator's cooling capacity. I suppose some sort of a compromise should be attempted, where the heater stops the feet from icing up, yet demists the screen, whilst those increasingly evident eyeball fresh-air aeroflow vents can be used to blast outside fresh air into a driver's face, thus doing much to keep him well and truly on the ball. These vents are easier to direct than quarter-lights, which so often tend to get in the way of a driver's knuckles. The screen must not demist up on the move as there just may not be time for either crew member to be able to break off from their own specialised duties to wipe the screen over. If it becomes necessary, then the number two should do this. Invariably this must mean that a safety-belt will have had to be undone whilst the wiping is carried out, so it is quite obviously not a good plan. A session with a demist cloth just before the start is the best preventive trick.

THE RIGHT FOOD

In addition to being prepared with drop-off preventives, it is as well to make sure that the right food is consumed prior to the event. Even driving a rally car over a demanding and undulating route induces considerable movement of the stomach. A large plate of fried or fancy food, just before the off is hardly the best start to any night. A driver ought to eat well in preparation for his night on the move, but the right type of food must be chosen. It is also as well to carry certain basic and easily stored foods on board any rally car, as long as these do not get in the way whilst on the move. On the longer events, it may be that the catering arrangements are few and far between anyway. A supply of liquid of a non-fizzy sort, or Thermos flasks of tea or coffee are a good plan, but the contents of these must be drunk sparingly if the driver wants to be able to stay at the wheel for long periods of time without having to stop for obvious reasons every now and again. Drinking fluids must also be stored safely so their containers do not become broken as Thermos flasks unfortunately can become smashed, and glass bottles rolling across the back seat have a habit of breaking. The best containers for liquid refreshments are plastic bottles, and even so these should be really securely stored.

Boiled sweets that can be sucked are about the best temporary sustainers for rallyists work. Chocolate is very sensible too but from personal experience, this does tend to make one thirsty. Toffee ought to be avoided as this can accelerate toothache. There are of course some folk who cannot concentrate without chewing gum. Well, if this helps, there can be little wrong with taking plenty of gum along. The obvious snag is swallowing the wretched stuff, if there is a major aerobatic excursion, or should I say, unscheduled flight. Chewing gum has been most useful to patch up many a rally car's sump or petrol tank, so perhaps every well prepared driver ought to ensure that he equips himself with a few packets. There is certainly no point in taking along loads of picnic equipment or piles of sandwiches. There are usually organised catering arrangements especially for rally crews on most rallies. Anyway, the communal bun fight occasions are all very much a part of the sport. Sandwiches usually land up in soggy heaps on the car floor or destroy themselves all over the seats. So do not bother to take food along with you in preparation for a siege. The only good things about taking food with you on the way to a rally start, which is a long way from base, are that it saves a crew's pennies, as well as being quicker than waiting to be served in roadside establishments. But once actually on the event, the least encumbrances in the cockpit the better.

If car sickness rears its ugly head, and it can with drivers on rallies, then Marzine or Kwells or such like ought to be on hand just in case. It is most probable that a co-driver will have some with him anyway. But here again, some care ought to be exercised, as some anti-car sickness tablets do tend to induce drowsiness. It has been known for drivers, who have already taken some types of stay-awake pills to react most strangely when they have taken an anti-sickness pill as well. Obviously, it is so much more satisfactory if a driver can drive on rallies without having to resort to taking any pills at all. But if this is not possible, then he ought to make sure that the pills he does take do go together, and that by trying them out before the rally, no peculiar effects take place. Your doctor should be able to advise on whether a certain pill will be compatible with another.

Aids to driver comfort, as long as they do not take up too much room in the rally car should be encouraged. Rally drivers, who are completely comfortable, are invariably likely to put up a better performance than those who are distracted by discomforts of one sort or another. For the early morning glare, or low sun conditions, then sunglasses must be taken along by drivers. These ought to be Polaroid ones, as there is less likelihood of any distortion of the road ahead. To avoid these fairly expensive glasses becoming broken by safety belts crushing them or being sat upon, a stout spectacle case is a wise purchase. I have seen many rally cars firmly planted straight on at a sharp bend into the sun, usually at the end of a straight. The driver could not see the corner. Dark glasses also help a driver's eyes become more quickly used to dusk, as well as lessening eye fatigue in the early mornings too. Again for the eyes, or the protection of same, a pair of goggles ought to be taken along by each crew member, particularly the driver. For, if the screen was to be smashed in an inversion or severe body distortion, then a driver might have to continue driving to stay in a rally without a screen, his eyes braving the elements, as I well know having driven (after a roll) many forest stages on one RAC Rally without a screen, during which time I was periodically showered with rocks every time I was overtaken.

COSMETICS

Lips, even in warm and comfortable saloon cars, tend to become very sore if a driver is unused to the rigours of nocturnal weather. It is as well to take along one of those sticks of lip ointment to prevent chapping. On really cold rallies, and especially if the cockpit is known to be a really chilly place, then Nivea or a cold cream of similar type is quite a good idea. This can be rubbed onto the lower part of the face. It helps to ward off frostbite, which could happen in freezing fog without a screen. Rubbing on cream of this type before rallies is to be recommended for people who have a very sensitive skin anyway. All this attention to matters cosmetic may well seem to be effeminate, but if these things help, even in a small way, to make a rally driver more comfortable, then he is more likely to be able to give of his best. Many of these tips are fiddling and time absorbing; their overall advantage, however, is undeniable and their cost minimal, especially when compared to the overall cost of fielding a rally car and crew, even for the humblest night rally.

CLOTHES

As to what a driver should wear? This is really a very personal decision. It is as well to wear overalls though, not necessarily the lightweight racing suits, for though these are fireproof, which with today's increasing rally speeds is no bad thing, they tend to be too flimsy for being able to withstand sessions of screwing the car back together again, changing wheels, and pushing exhaust systems back in place. Thick drill ones on the other hand become too heavy for comfortable fast driving, very quickly becoming sodden with sweat. Those heavy mechanic types of overalls also take much longer to dry out than the racing versions after a driver has emerged from lying in a puddle. Somewhere between the two varieties of overall there are some racing mechanics' overalls which are stout enough to stand up to their wearers working on cars, look as if they may withstand frequent washings through, yet are sufficiently light not to be uncomfortable if a driver, thus garbed, really was to get down to some swift motoring. The best kit for a rally driver is certainly a pair of one-piece zip-up overalls, with flameproof Nomex long-johns underneath. The outer garments should be equipped with plenty of pockets, though make sure no hard or sharp objects are stored therein. Maybe a spare pair for changing into on the longer events might be sensible. To top these should go the universal rallyman's uniform of a rally jacket, anyway about the most sensible top coat to wear. These I have found best with a Velcro touch and close fastener at the front. There is nothing more annoying than trying to sort out a zip fastener with one hand at below freezing temperatures, although a zip at least does not snag on woollens or nylons like the Velcro hooks do. However, this latter feature maybe hardly relevant on these pages. Such a rally jacket should be selected with a hood too, because it often happens that there is likely to be a fair amount of standing about to be done, often in really stormy conditions. A hood also helps when there are a few minutes available to snatch some shut-eye, as a driver can curl up inside his hood and so get away from all those bright lights. The possibility must always be faced, that the rally might just end up with a long walk for one or both crew members. So, although a sheepskin might be warmer, these do not dry out so quickly once wet, are not washable like a rally jacket, and are certainly not so expendable. There are many rally jackets on the market, in most cases built specially for the job of making the rally driver's lot as comfortable as possible. One of these ought to be at the top of any rallyist's Christmas present list.

I always think gloves are important too. Admittedly, with so many sports steering wheels now being produced with leather covered rims, the first essential of driving gloves giving adequate steering wheel rim grip is now no longer as important, but the back of a driving glove is most useful for wiping the inside of the screen. Also I have even been able to put out a fire thanks to wearing driving gloves, as well as finding them invaluable for wiring up smouldering exhaust pipes without having my hands scorched. The best gloves to wear are those with chamois leather backs to them, rather than the string ones. I have found them a great help if I have been driving a car which was plagued with steering feed-back on the rough. The general cushioning effect that they produce helps on the longer events to cut down the possibility of blisters. All in all essential clothing.

To complete a driver's comfort equipment, it is as well to take along a pillow and a rug, if the event is of such length that sleep is going to be required. A driver only needs a few minutes deep sleep every few hours and he can keep going for days. The amount of room taken up and the weight of these items is negligible and besides, they are a real Godsend if a crew has to retire in the wilderness. Even though any well designed rally jacket should be warm enough for the worst conditions, it might be as well to take along a pullover; again the room taken up is minimal. A groundsheet should be packed on board too, just in case crew members have to lie on the ground to work on the underside of their steed. Such a sheet can be used to stop some of the other equipment rattling on the move, and by saving rallyists from puddles and mire, helps to keep them dry.

HELMETS

With more and more rallies, however humble in status, using one or more special stages in their formula, most rally drivers are going to need to purchase a crash helmet sooner or later. The original 'top-knot' acorn shaped affairs would seem to be now finally out of fashion. Surprisingly the crash helmet is about the only item of personal kit that must be worn on any major rally, and indeed such equipment is usually scrutineered at the start these days. Helmets must be of the latest type to comply with the new rules governing what specification of helmet is allowed. They must be capable of giving full temple protection, complying with the British Standards Institute's specifications 1869 or 2495, or meet the similar requirements laid out by the Snell Memorial Foundation in the United States. These requirements have been evolved as a result of very rigorous tests, the usual procedure being the dropping of weights on four selected parts of a helmet, mounted for the purpose on a dummy head-form, the force transmitted to the form being measured in lbs. These four sites are the front, rear and both sides, the helmets having to withstand a penetration test as well, carried out by the dropping of a spike onto the shell. As a matter of interest, and to prove the whole need for all this trouble, for a crash hat to be awarded the BSI 2495 ticket, it has to be able to withstand no less than a 5,000 lbs force, transmitted to the dummy's head when in a 150 ft/lbs collision with the shell.

As a crash helmet has to be strong and rigid, but still light enough to be practical over a long distance, most of the present competition helmets are made from aircraft quality glassfibre cloth bonded with special high impact resin, while the lining usually consists of non-resilient plastic foam, about an inch or so thick, which acts as quite an effective impact absorber. The very best and most expensive helmets also include a middle layer, consisting of a thin layer of slow return springy material, offering the wearer additional impact protection, as well as protecting the non-resilient shell in a minor impact. Inside the best helmets, there should be nylon-covered foam padding, and in the more expensive versions flameproof material as padding.

Although the very best helmets that money can buy are those all-enveloping types, such as the legendary Bell Star, virtually uniform for so many of the top racing drivers, verbal communication does tend to become muffled and they are rather stuffy in a closed rally car. A word of advice on the subject is then in order. Do not rush out to buy a particular helmet merely because your favourite Grand Prix driver wears a similar version, or just because it might be the most suitable colour for carrying on the back window-ledge in between rallies! The helmet chosen must, above all else, be comfortable. It should not be excessively heavy as there is nothing worse than being weighed down for the best part of a night's special stages with a helmet that is too heavy for your neck muscles. Again, all too often the straps fitted to many helmets may be just fine for tearing round Brands Hatch on a Sunday afternoon, but can rasp most uncomfortably if worn for very long. Choose an American-styled wrap-round-the-ears helmet by all means, but select one with a really adequate jaw spreading piece, as well as a thick under-chin strap. It is a good idea to retain the clip-on peak which is extremely useful to save the face from a painful knock in a severe jolt. These peaks may look as if they are only really of any use to ward off the sun's glare but surprisingly can prove to be a boon in an accident.

There used to be a tip that many of the works drivers used to adopt, of cutting a series of holes in the sides of their helmets and ear pieces so that they could be better able to hear their fellow crew member's verbal communication, especially the directional instructions. But scrutineers can turn down helmets so modified, so perhaps such tips should be referred to only in the past tense for the newcomer. But with present-day rally cars, often devoid of padding, under-carpets, and the like, the level of cockpit noise has risen appreciably. Actually being able to hear, and indeed to make oneself heard in a competitive rally car in action, is often a problem. If helmets are worn for long periods of time, at least the considerable fatigue angle of noise may well be partially overcome, but there is no quicker way for a navigator to go hoarse. The noise inside can be really high when exhaust manifolds and systems become knocked up to resonate against a bodyshell on a rough event, as well as the added decibel ingredient of flying rocks bouncing off the underside of a car's floor and scraping the underneath of a low-slung car. Starting off in the higher echelons of the sport, the professionals very quickly adopted intercoms to combat the noise problem, similar to those used in aircraft cockpits. These days, not only do all the factory teams use them, or modern lightweight derivatives, but many top private entrants have equipped themselves with sets too—but more about such

4 If a driver trys hard enough, he will eventually make an unscheduled departure from the intended route! With luck, there will be spectators around to lift him back. If not, he and his co-driver should anchor up their tow rope in readiness for somebody to generously tow them back on.

5 Saab have been at the top of the sport for many years, first with their tiny two-stroke engined cars and more recently with their V4 models. They are blessed with good ground clearance, large wheels, the traction advantages of front-wheel drive, and an extremely strong bodyshell. This Swedish crew are keeping in touch with each other over the noise of howling exhaust, and flying stones against the underside, by use of an intercom set, now virtually considered standard equipment for the aspiring International Rallyist.

equipment when cockpit preparation is discussed later, as well as how to use it, when pace-note reading is covered.

Undoubtedly, a number one aid for any rally driver is a really comfortable but secure seat. Many sporting production cars are now fitted with extremely well thought out seats today, there being no need to substitute these for one of the many so-called rally style seats on the market. Invariably, the seats that seem to fill every accessory shop window in the land might look the part, but are far too flimsy for serious rally use, being made in the main from flexible glassfibre affixed to flimsy tubular sub-frames.

For a driver, there is not the same necessity as his passenger to need a reclining seat, but what he does need is a seat that holds him really securely in his place when his car is sliding sideways, and possibly leaping over undulations at the same time. Especially if the standard seat is a tip forward one, to allow access to the rear seat for a two-door model, it should be battened down so that the back is fixed to the floor. In the unfortunate event of an involuntary inversion a driver would not want to have his seat swing down from the floor forcing him against the safety belts to such an extent that the release mechanism would have an exaggerated task. A reclining seat, with headrest, is best for the navigator's side of the car but here again, modifications to seats and the various seating alternatives will be covered later in car preparation.

BELTS

Safety belts are a very personal thing. Even though they are now a legal necessity for a new car, the wearing of them is entirely up to the individual. There are statistics that show fairly con-clusively that the wearing of belts does help to reduce the possibility of serious injury in an accident. So presumably, even in a rally accident, this would also be true. But there are some of the best rally drivers in the business who do not wear belts: though I would say that this is becoming a slightly dated view. Maybe the statistical evidence is now so strongly in favour of belts or the speeds becoming so high, that the principle criticism of belts being restrictive for a driver throwing a car about, is

C

being overcome by commonsense. Although the very best belts, with which to equip any rally car, are full-harness ones, many drivers prefer to just use the lap ones. Thus secured, a driver may find the increased body movement more comfortable for negotiating intricate situations, and more convenient for road sections in particular. He could then always revert to using the full shoulder straps as well on the special stages. Certainly, when a crewmember wants to have a few minutes shut-eye whilst having his partner take over the wheel, whatever his views on the wearing of belts, he should tighten the lap strap right up. Even in the most smoothly driven rally car, complete relaxation and the possibility of sleep without the restraint of a belt of some nature is likely to be difficult.

From personal experience, I have had two rolls and three fairly severe head-ons, including my World Cup Yugoslavian lorry shunt in a rally car. Each time I had the good fortune to be wearing a well designed full-harness belt, properly adjusted and each time, I have been lucky enough to walk away from the accident. Although, on one Scottish Rally it was not exactly easy, as the Mini I was driving landed in the upper branches of a Drumtochty tree, some considerable way down a hillside, after a brake failure. In fact, the most dangerous part of this alarming incident, and there are likely to be many in store for any rally-man, was regaining terra firma.

SMOKING

I would not recommend a driver to smoke during the most hectic sessions of any rally. I bring forward no scientific or health reason against this. It's just that if you did happen to have a shunt, or even such a near moment that a lighted cigarette were to become knocked out of the mouth to fall around the inside of the car, things might just warm up a little too much. I hate to think what might have happened in shunts I have known if either crew member had been smoking just before their inversion. It is a miracle anyway why more rally cars do not go up in smoke when sparks fly near split petrol tanks, without the additional, yet avoidable, risk of there being lighted cigarettes as well. In any case smoking on special stages which involve traversing Forestry Commission land will, on most events, be punishable by exclusion from the results.

However if you have to smoke, and many leading rally drivers do because it is best to be as relaxed as possible, go ahead. Incidentally, the footwell in any car Pat Moss used to drive would invariably be ankle-deep in nub-ends a works mechanic told me; an obvious case for king-sized ashtrays. But do ensure that by smoking you do not have to reach all over the car. Lay on the necessary lighter and ashtray as much to hand as possible. There are even machines on the market that, by selecting a button, a lighted cigarette is passed out to a driver on an illuminated tray. This means that he does not have to take his eyes off the road at all during the manoeuvre of lighting-up. Fumbling for a light is absolutely out in any rally car—a dangerous facet to bad preparation. But, if you are a driver who cannot concentrate without a smoke, then remember, in the cause of the very best crew relationship, that maybe your co-driver is a non-smoker. So a continuous stream of foul cigarette smoke might make his ride with you even more uncomfortable than would be the case if he merely had to put up with your driving.

A TEAM GAME

Before I go into what makes a rally driver tick, it is as well to emphasise that he is a part of a team. He must therefore understand the problems involved on the other side of the cockpit. The duties should be sorted out before ever embarking on an event. When there is a puncture or the car goes off the road, each crew member should know exactly what he should do—if he has the choice! One so often sees novice crews both rushing to the spare wheel, both trying to get hold of the wheelbrace and, once they've fought over these, finally scrapping over who should wind up the jack. It is such a simple job to work out in advance who does what in such a case. Then there is no crowding and, what is more important, no waste of precious time.

A driver should definitely practice wheelchanges with his fellow crew member, until the movements are really well tuned, and there is no fumbling. Seconds lost making a mess of a wheelchange by the roadside are often extremely difficult to win back once on the go again. Time lost is lost for good, if penalties have once been collected. The same goes for the order of operations that will take the least time. All likely jobs, such as a fanbelt change or tighten up, ought to be rehearsed. Nor at any brief stop in a rally, should both crew members chat away to the crowd, sign autographs or buy postcards for Great Aunts, if the few minutes in hand could be more usefully employed checking the car over. The various checks can be pre-assigned so easily : it is surprising how very quickly two can go round a rally car to check oil, clean lamps and screens, check tyre wall and tread condition, and still find time to down a cup of tea.

From the start, the captaincy of any crew ought to be decided. I have already said that a driver should run the car; a co-driver, the office aspects of an entry. So, if the event is run to time, as all rallies are, then it is the number two who should be ' Number One '. He is nearer to the time anyway.

A driver will drive better if he knows, by regular checks where he has time, that his car is in decent fettle. There are those who think it is better for a driver to know nothing about what sort of a state his car is in. Well, I disagree with this view. Rallying is too dangerous for games to be played where the safety of a crew, marshals, or even other road users is at stake. If there is anything wrong with a rally car, then the driver really ought to know all about it. I subscribe to the view, that a driver, by knowing all is well, is likely to be able to concentrate on his driving more effectively than one who is continually worrying about his master cylinder level, or whether his oil level is dangerously low.

THE RIGHT SPANNERS

Just the right tools ought to be carried, of which more anon, and the crew should know exactly which spanner will fit which nut. It really is a great help for any rally driver to understand how to fix the sort of faults that are likely to crop up during an event. Roger Clark, perhaps Britain's finest rally driver, once confirmed this necessity for a rallyist by saying " When you hear a noise, you know where to look ". Knowing where to look for a fault saves time and can, by the crew fixing it and carefully nursing the car on to the next point where there may be time for servicing, keep a car in the hunt.

If you are going to go rallying from the driver's seat, then you must decide, before you ever set forth, whether you are taking part just for amusement, or have aspirations towards the award's list. No doubt many start rallying purely as a sport. Then, after any success, some change their attitude to dedication and a single-mindedness to win. It has to be faced, if you are going to be trying, then sooner or later you will have an accident and as speeds of competitive rally cars go up, it is more than likely to be a big one. It is all very well saying do not run before you can walk. This applies to begin with certainly but, after a while, you will learn no more—unless you start to try. Only by trying will you ever be able to tell if you have what it really takes to make a winning rally driver. Along the way, there will be accidents.

I can remember when a young Yorkshire car salesman caused quite a sensation by really flying into the awards lists regularly, though equally regularly he flew off the road too. He was quickly dubbed ' Crasher '; his name, Tony Fall, whose prowess at the wheel of everything from a factory Mini Cooper S in the old Abingdon days, an Italian Lancia, Datsuns of one sort and another, and a World Cup London to Mexico Escort has become legendary.

The top team boss in professional rallying, Stuart Turner, once said " You can't have tried, unless you have had accidents. But it is he who goes on having them who is never likely to win ".

Of course the attitude of the factory team driver is likely to be different in the final reckoning from that of the amateur, who is more likely to be paying his own bills. These days, with increased competition and so many events being won by seconds, the outright win is becoming all that matters. So the motto for the best drivers has now become, often under the orders of having a go at putting up the fastest special stage times possible, ' Win or Bust '. It is therefore rather unfair when a top driver then earns himself a reputation of being a car breaker. Finishing surprisingly does not seem to matter in the higher realms of the sport these days. A driver's reputation, and so his market value, can be seriously affected by putting up stage times that are not on the top ten leader board.

Sometimes, works teams field a car purely for development. This is never very popular with a professional driver, especially as usually there is little likelihood of the car ever making it to the finish—even before it starts!

If you are to succeed as a rally driver, then you must have the will to win, or should I say not to lose. Some up-and-coming rally drivers often earn themselves a bad name from their less ambitious rivals by being bad losers. Being a bad loser is not such a bad quality. In the words of that oracle of rallying, Eric Carlsson " You should mind losing. If you don't care about it, you shouldn't start!" Such a view on driving should not be taken too far though, because although you should never want to lose, becoming angry and vicious at the wheel affects a driver's judgement, and might just prove to be prohibitively expensive. Somewhere along the line lies the right attitude. To succeed, whether amateur or professional status is being pursued, calls for a mixture of tiger and self control.

Confidence in the other crew member's activities are a prerequisite for an harmonious partnership. A driver must feel safe when following the instructions of his partner. He must be able to believe those instructions without question.

FINANCE AND INSURANCE

Also, it is very important to sort out before the start exactly what the financial arrangements are. How the costs before, during, and after every event are split between the crew need to be discussed and sorted out. Try to be optimistic as well. You never know, somebody has to win. So decide how prize and bonus money will be shared out in advance. As a rule, with a navigator doing the paperwork, it works best if on the smaller events he pays the entry fee and buys the maps whilst the driver buys all the petrol and is responsible for preparing his car as well as paying for the inevitable restoration afterwards! On the larger events the entry fees will be very much more, so a fifty-fifty share out on all running costs works best.

Insurance can so often be ignored, or rather taken for granted. If this does happen, then it is more than likely that a situation will arise when a claim does occur. It is essential for each rally car to be adequately insured, even if the budget can only stretch to effecting legal cover. Completely comprehensive insurance, particularly on special stages, is likely to put most competitors, with a budget of normal dimensions, well into the red, but both crew members should be insured to drive the rally car, the exact liability of one to another in the car being understood. Most insurance companies will preclude passenger liability, so it is wise for this to be negotiated separately if injury and hospitalisation is likely to be much of a financial problem. A serious accident is always unfortunately on the cards.

Special stages are regarded by insurance companies in the same light as racing, which judging by today's competitive speeds, may not be an unfair comparison. A standard motor policy will exclude cover when the policy holder uses his vehicle for ' racing, pacemaking, reliability trials, speed testing or rallies '. An extension of each individual driver's policy is a matter, of course, for individual negotiation. However, there is a scheme available through organising clubs, which exists to provide short period cover for drivers on the road sections of Closed, Restricted and National events, as well as a further scheme to provide cover for Internationals. Details can be obtained from the RAC Motor Sport Division's official brokers, C. T. Bowring and Muir Bedall (Home) Ltd., The Bowring Building, Tower Place, London EC3.

The most usual cover taken by competitors rallying today is comprehensive for the public road sections and legal cover against third party claims on the special stages. Also, whilst taking part in any event held under an RAC permit, which includes special stages, a competitor will be jointly indemnified with the promoters and other competitors up to an amount of £1,000,000, for any one accident, in respect of his liabilities for death or bodily injury to persons and for damage to private property. Cover for this sort of risk is taken out by the organisers.

The importance of sorting out this insurance properly before the off cannot be emphasised enough. This has become even more important lately because of the seriousness of an offence in this sector, the authorities taking an exceedingly dim view of motoring insurance offences.

THE DRIVING ART

One could almost devote a whole book to the art of rally driving. There was once a time when it sufficed for the rallyist to merely cope with each and every skid, or try to, when they happened. But today's technique is very different. You only have to observe the experts at work to realise that a rally car on the limit is in one big continuous slide. The slide is often very slight—but it is deliberate. The school for this sort of thing was dubbed in the beginning as being the Scandinavian technique.

Now a great deal of ' brouhaha ' has blown up about the way Scandinavian rally drivers are able to drive so quickly. Their basic advantage is not some peculiarity of their stock, but simply that they have had loose surfaces as their natural motoring background since the first day they took the wheel of their family's car. Having to take a variable road surface into account every time they take a car out does not worry them in the same way as it would an ordinary British driver. Whether the slippery nature of the surface is gravel, grit after the winter snows, or whether a journey is undertaken in the height of winter, coping becomes second nature to these Norsemen.

By the same token, as driving in conditions that would normally be rated by even the most ardent British motoring enthusiast as a challenge, they do not present anything out of the ordinary to a Swede especially as he, in a nation of drivers, will most likely have been driving just as soon as he was legally able. So those with access to private land to try out driving techniques, at a pre-legal driving age, are more likely to be labelled as naturals. Men of the calibre of Andrew Cowan came to rallying from a farming environment, and even the late Jim

Clark, who was also one of the finest rally drivers in the Border country before he ever took up racing, obviously benefited from being able to handle a vehicle's controls at an early age.

Many drivers may feel that they can drive as quickly as the next man on tarmac, saying that relative performances on events are all a matter of he who has the fastest car must win the day. This is nonsense on most rally sections. Obviously, if tyres, brakes, reactions and the brake horsepower of the engine were all equal, if this were possible, it might be the case; but the human element is likely to sort out an order of prowess. On most rally routes, what tarmac there is will most likely be unseen, and at least peppered with gravel, to make even this effectively a loose surface when taken at the limit.

LOOSE SURFACE MASTERY

As most rallies usually have loose surface sections in their make-up, either in the form of special stages or rough tracks as the most challenging parts of the road section, then being able to cope with such an ordeal at competitive speeds is a priority for the rally driver. Being able to take loose surfaces in his stride, almost as second nature, should be the goal of every novice.

After very little experience it soon becomes apparent that it is better to have the car in a slide, or varying degrees of slide, rather than merely do something with the steering wheel if the latest tyres were to let him down, the brakes allowed his car to enter a corner quicker than planned, or the corner in sight (for some extraordinary reason known only to nature) suddenly turned out to be a bend in the opposite direction from the way it looked. In the same way that a skier feels his direction and speed by turning himself on his skis sideways to the fall of the slope, so a rally driver on the limit can edge the tyres against the forward motion by swinging the car around its axis. In this way, it is less likely that a driver will lose either end of his vehicle, and if he should do so he will stand a better chance of being able to do something about it. He would be in control of the whole, as opposed to winning back in line either end in turn.

It takes a great deal of practice to develop a style of driving that is smooth. In the early days, much time can be wasted and incidents actually be made worse, by a driver allowing the car to swing to excess from side to side. Over-enthusiasm, it goes without labouring, can all too easily put a rally car off the road. If a car is allowed to become too sideways and the brakes applied in panic, then the experiment might well conclude with a roll. Still, there is always the first time I suppose.

By playing a car versus the road surface, feeling what things are like, through the tyres, it will quickly be realised that only in this way will the effect of reactions, coping with a change of direction over a blind brow, be more likely to be able to keep a car on the road. With practice, a driver will soon develop a technique that will be automatic and he will not have to think about every slide, or should we say, the long continuous slide. He should have then mastered the other essential movements that go along with the controlled weaving: changing gear to the power curve of the engine's maximum advantage; braking smoothly; and looking ahead.

It is a well-used criticism of British rally drivers, even the best ones who have weaned themselves on Welsh lanes, that they spend far too much time buzzing along in low gears, worrying about the immediate corner with which they are confronted. They simply drive on their gears, tyres and brakes. As a result, put them onto a fast Alpine section and they will travel kilometres slower than their Continental rivals. Only by looking ahead at the bend after the one that is in front can miles per hour be built up. This thinking ahead, coupled with the controlled continuous slide will really do much to build a driver's speed up. The very best way to cure this habit of braking too often, always the most usual fault in any novice, is to rally a car that is so slow, or down on engine power, that only by infrequent braking will the car stay in the rally at all, let alone do sections in the time allowed. In the days when Eric Carlsson used to stagger the motoring world with his performances in his tiny two stroke 850cc Saab, more often than not achieving times considerably quicker than Porsches, and even works Austin Healey 3000s, he was well known for his very rare use of the brake pedal. The maxim with a slower car must be, that once you have taken so long building your speed up, the very last thing you really want to do is to cut this back by a subconscious stab at the brake pedal. By looking ahead, using all the road, and braking only if it is not possible to cope with a particular hazard that might present itself, the very slowest car can always put up surprisingly fast times, even in the face of the near racing specification engines that are being purchased by rank novices.

NO LIFTING OFF

Whilst all this emphasis is being made on not braking, it is also important to change the habit of lifting off, or stealing the occassional sneak lift of foot. To begin with, this will be difficult. A concentrated effort will have to be made as it often costs as much time as a straight forward brake. The time taken over a section can so often be reduced without any increase in risk simply by mastering the inherent natural urge in any sane driver of wanting to brake as well as lifting the right foot off just in case. On this subject, Stirling Moss, who once was a very successful Coupes des Alpes driver, theorised one further about rally driving when he said ' Any time when you are not using the throttle or the brakes is a waste of time '. The need to be positive about feet movement is worth bearing in mind.

Further to having the most comfortable driving position possible, it is a boon to be able to see the front corners of the car, particularly over twisty territory. The driver should not select a low-down lie-back driver's seat. With a more sensible high-up seating position, he will be more able to place his car better on the road, as well as being able to spot the odd rocky outcrop, hole in the road, or log a little sooner.

The pedals must be really accessible too, preferably with meaty pads on them, and modified if necessary so that toe-heeling is a natural movement. The recent craze for people to say that they favour clutchless gearchanging has little point, unless in the direst emergency. It will not matter how expert a driver thinks he is at synchronising his engine to road speed, it is not giving even the strongest transmission much of a chance. As far as a gearchanging code is concerned, I would not subscribe to the rule that double declutching should be the best order of the day. This is a technique that certainly ought to be known, just in case the synchromesh packs up on a longer event, but never ponderously practised I would have thought by present-day serious drivers.

But the biggest fault of any novice rally driver, and indeed his worst habit, is usually panic braking. Invariably, it ends up with one very bent motor car. The tell-tale streaks of black rubber into sharp bends are a sure sign on any rally of many an accident that should by all the laws of gravity and over-reaction have happened. Only experience, and rally driving reactions cultivated until they become natural, rather than meticulously worked out, will cure the habit. After a while, a driver it is hoped, will try whatever the odds to make the turn, rather than merely slam his anchors on to disappear straight on at a T junction, or over a bank at the entry of a corner.

LEFT FOOT BRAKING

When other techniques have been mastered the expert will eventually be able to experiment in the realms of left-foot braking, of which a great deal of vague nonsense has been expounded. As a logical extension of using the brakes as little as possible, left-foot braking only becomes essential as a way to reduce a car's speed enough to make a sudden bend.

Left-foot braking came from those Scandinavian rally aces again. It is balancing the braking effect of the brakes against the accelerative forces achieved by the accelerator. This all sounds very contradictory. It is. However going back to the essential art of a rally driver being able to feel his car's axis, to then be able to pivot his car around that axis on the move, the next step is to introduce left-foot braking as well to assist in the control of this manoeuvre. If the car is a front-wheel drive effort, the front wheels are driven under power, the brakes work on all four wheels (it is assumed!), so if the drive is left engaged instead of a declutch being carried out by the driver under braking and the brakes are pushed on against the drive

the tail can be made to move out, whilst the front is still being
pulled by the engine around the corner. By increasing or reducing the power of the engine versus the effects of the brakes,
different results can be made to happen. Such a technique is
most useful in front-wheel drive cars, but as an aid to very
daring reduction of corner entering speeds in most rally cars,
it is the only safe way to stay in business. If the brakes are
applied carefully, neither end of any two-wheel drive car will
in fact lock-up, the driving effect of the driving wheels will be
sufficient to avoid a lock-up. About the only snag with this
advanced method of driving quickly is that the working
temperatures of the brakes are going to be increased, which
is hardly surprising. Any rally car is bound to have had anti-
fade competition brake-lining materials fitted, but, even so,
brake fluid boiling and the cooking of brake hydraulic seals
can occur.

Left-foot braking naturally works best on ice and snow.
Indeed, only by mastering this technique can anybody hope to

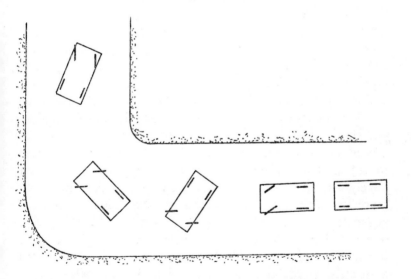

1 Setting the car up for a corner: first the driver steers in the
opposite direction to the corner, and then flicks the whole car the
other way to negotiate the bend

drive (and what is more important, stop) safely on ice with standard tyres. The earlier snow drivers of note all used to cadence brake; the technique of stamping the brakes on and off to slow the wheels up, and then release them before they locked up. But ' left-foot ' has superceded this in top-class rally driving nowadays. Even in the sophisticated world of studs on winter rallies, all the loose surface techniques still apply, only the speeds are higher.

Following on from being able to swing the car about its axis, this way and that, as well as being able to play power against brakes, comes the realisation, as with skiing, of being able to use the sideways movement of the car to do two things. Firstly, to slow up the car's progress on loose surfaces to just the right speed in the shortest possible time and distance before each corner and secondly, to edge the car purposefully into a slide, the contrary way to the direction of the corner that confronts the driver. This latter action must seem strange to the novice. But, take one look at any of the masters at work and you will see that they all seem to swing their cars the other way, sideways to the direction of the bend they are rushing up to. This is all deliberate. It is a most useful way to scrub excess speed off, to flick the car into the set-up attitude, and, at the same time, to have selected the right gear and concluded the braking in one rapid and automatic action.

There are various other useful tricks of the trade that some people have used with success from time to time. Colin Malkin, one time British Rally Champion and number two driver to Cowan on his winning London to Sydney Marathon drive, used to use his handbrake a great deal on the move. He did not merely use the handbrake in the Driving Test style either, to cause the back end of his vehicle to slide round violently to negotiate tricky hairpin turns, or to enter really sharp side turnings. Nor did he use it exclusively to turn round in a hurry in a narrow place if a navigator had gone wrong or if he dared to overshoot. Malkin, particularly with his rear-wheel drive Imp, used to apply the handbrake as a ' left-foot ' braking method against his engine's power. He preferred the feel of using the handbrake apparently, as he found that the foot brake tended to lock-up the fairly light front end with a subsequent loss of steering.

Left-foot braking does not work at all well on rear-wheel drive cars, whose front ends are too heavy. It works best on well balanced cars, and must become totally standard practice if the current vogue for mid-engined cars blossoms into an overall trend. It is perhaps as well here to say that the left foot with this technique should be kept on or near the brake pedal, apart from dashes across the floor for the odd stab at the clutch, whilst the right foot works the throttle. But playing with the brakes has to be watched, particularly if the road is full of hummocks. Those who saw the famous Castrol film on the Thousand Lakes will have seen what can all too easily happen if the brakes are applied in the air. In the film, a Volvo comes to a very expensive conclusion proving this point, as well as the requirement for no steering to be on when the car lands.

I once rolled a Mini on an RAC end over end. The reason was not because I had applied any steering in flight, but because I must have been caught unawares, and steadied myself on the brake pedal during the launch. As I landed fairly hard, I pushed the brakes on even harder. The car tripped on its nose into the track's surface to cartwheel into component form. I had learned yet another lesson.

Brace yourself, on Special Stages in particular, so that you can be in complete control of your pedals, even when the car is being violently thrown from bump to bump. Ideally, side support pads ought to be affixed in a well prepared rally cockpit for the sides of a drivers' legs, as well as a rest bar for his left foot when it is not required to do anything. These mods will do much to avoid the potentially dire consequences of a driver's legs flailing about. It might also help to add a cycle handlebar grip to the handbrake, as well as welding on an extension to improve the leverage. This may well be necessary anyway if the seating position has been altered from standard. Any handbrake in a rally car should be well maintained. It is a very important piece of apparatus, the action of which should be fly-on fly-off, so that the push-button lock-on does not waste any time. Along with the left-foot method, the setting up of a rally car the wrong way to the corner's direction, looking ahead, and concentrating on speed achieved, the full potential of the handbrake too, in a particular rally car, can only become totally second nature after a great deal of practice. The big snag with practising is that it can really only be carried out properly on events themselves. Such activities have to be expensive.

Pacing yourself is another facet of this demanding sport. It has often been said that the most cunning driver is the one who knows just how slow to go—to win. There is no point at all in roaring about the place on the link sections, if plenty of time has been allowed by the organisers. The car should be conserved, if there is no real need to go quickly.

6 The European aces rarely seem to use their brakes, yet seldom have accidents. They use all four wheels, moving the car sideways, to retard and line up their car for loose surface bends. That is what former European Rally Champion Harry Kallstrom and Gunnar Hagbom are doing here.

7 The trend for the future may well be mid-engined cars taking the top awards. One thing is certain, Rally cars will have to become lighter, faster, yet somehow stronger. Here, during what was obviously an adventurous run, the Porsche 914/6 mid-engined car of Claude Haldi and John Gretener treat a sheet of ice with apparent contempt.

8 The Scandinavians can usually be counted on to be the most spectacular. In this case an Opel Rallye Kadett, driven by Ove Eriksen with Hans Johanssen. Such sideways motoring for long periods requires frequent checks of tyre sidewalls.

3 Directing from the Hot Seat

The well-disciplined rally driver will know where and when to apply the maximum effort at the most appropriate time. Like a good actor, he will need directing. This directing is just one of the responsibilities of his number two, who can be a co-driver or a navigator, his or her qualities being for the most part identical, as well as being the same basically as a driver's. For the purpose of this book, there is a difference. As the first, for the majority the only, stage to co-driving for any number two is likely to be by way of club rally navigation, I shall deal with preparing for this task first.

The Navigator

To some, like Vic Elford for instance, navigating has been a means to an end, namely when funds permit, a graduation to the driver's seat, but there are exceptions to every rule and for the most part, navigators are navigators, and drivers are drivers. Although this generalisation implies that never the twain shall meet as far as both their highly specialised functions are concerned, it does mean that both must understand each other's job. Any rally crew that does not comprehend that rallying is a team effort will never click. It is this clicking, or harmonising, that is so vital, for spending hours cooped up in a confined rally cockpit together is the easiest way of breaking up a beautiful friendship. Therefore, it might be as well to put aside thoughts of taking along the wife or girl friend for a start, as such teams rarely prove to be successful. It helps for

D

any driver to have at least tried his hand at navigating, if for no other reason than the useful realisation of how difficult it really is.

At this juncture, it is as well to emphasise that it is a complete waste of time and money to take a rally car out on an event unless the navigation is up to scratch. More rallies have been lost than won by the actions of navigators. It is all very well tearing along the roughest road faster than every other car on an event if, by incompetent navigating, it turns out to be the wrong road!

For the out-and-out novice, it is difficult to attract a recognised top class navigator. Often the rank novice has to train himself taking along a keen rally friend, who may be trying his hand at the sport from the navigator's seat for the first time. Errors in the course of learning are therefore going to be natural but if mistakes continue to be a part of such a navigator's activity, then a driver, who takes his rallying at all seriously, must be cruel to be kind and declare an obvious redundancy. Deciding whether a navigator is going to be any good will not take long. He or she has the knack, or they haven't. The combined functions of being able to think clearly under pressure, with eyes down and look in at the maps, thinking ahead, worrying about time, looking up at the road every few seconds are a very real challenge to any enthusiast that considers himself level-headed. The task is not an easy one, and is usually devoid of glamour. The navigator is a backroom boy, although on British club rallies, he perhaps contributes more to the outcome of a rally's result than any other factor.

Although it is important for a navigator to be able to drive reasonably well, it is seldom necessary on a British club event for him to change sides of the car. In fact from experience, most navigators only ever drive their driver's car on the way home, when the driver thinks he should have a sleep. Often this is in readiness to be in fine form when the weary car staggers into the local's car park, the stories of the night's happening being told by him to a hushed bar crowd. It is fair to say that very few of the top British club navigators can drive quickly at all. Navigating to them is an end in itself and, conversely, very few of the better club rally drivers could win any awards by reading a map.

Of the many skills the novice navigator has to master, the basic essential is to learn to be able to read a map. His fluency has to be so proficient that reading the map becomes as easy to him as reading a book. The desired total familiarity with maps only comes with much practice and, as I have already said, if the basic aptitude is lacking, any amount of practice is going to be rather a waste of everybody's time.

But, let us assume that our subject has what it takes, or rather realises he has himself, which at least shows all-important self-confidence. Map reading is not just a matter of being able to spot what is a church or a pylon. It is being able to translate the features of the map into relevancy beneficial to causing his particular rally car to progress down the route as quickly as possible. Not too much information should be passed to a driver, not too little, but the right route must be the result. Thus knowing exactly which roads constitute the right route is a number one essential, and transmitting that information to the driver, in as helpful a way as possible, is the second.

Most club rally routes these days are pin-pointed by map references. Map reference must be completely understood. The maps used on the RAC recognised events are all Ordnance Survey ones, their scale being one inch to each mile, with each map or sheet having its own number. These maps (hereafter abbreviated—OS) are covered with thin lines which make up squares, all part of the overall National Grid. Along the edges of the OS maps are figures, running up to 100 and then repeating themselves. These squares, or units of latitude and longitude, are per kilometre. It is the relation of the figures along the bottom and top of each OS map with those along the side edges that gives each all-important map reference. Often, each reference on a rally is preceded by the particular map number, as a reference recurs every sixty miles or so. On the back of each OS map, if purchased in fold-up form, is a plan of all the OS maps covering the country, together with their various numbers.

A map reference has six figures, made up from the figures along the bottom/top followed by the figures up the sides of the map. This order is important. Most novice navigators adopt the slogan ' Along the corridor—up the stairs ', as being the easiest way to make sure the method is adhered to when plotting a map reference. The first two figures of a reference, read as a pair, refer to the kilometre square numbers along the bottom of the map, and the third figure is a sub-division of that square in tenths of a kilometre. Next come the figures from the square along the sides (' Up the stairs '), being figures four and five of the reference. The last figure is the sub-division in tenths of the particular kilometre square. Plotting each reference is just a matter of tieing up the reading along the bottom or top of the map, with the reading along the sides. By accurately pin-pointing the two, the exact map reference can be determined. Once this simple routine can be done quickly then, in theory anyway, most British club events can be tackled. The map reference is the basis to British navigating lingo. Sometimes, six figure references will not be enough, especially if in the area there are a mass of minor tracks, so eight figure references can be used by the organisers. This merely means that figures four and eight are further subdivisions of the tenths of the kilometre squares, or in such cases hundredths.

ROMERS

There are a couple of tricks that are essential for any navigator in order to plot references as quickly and as accurately as possible. Firstly, a Romer will be needed. This is simply a small plastic device with scales marked on at least two sides. It is used by locating the square first by the ' Along the corridor, up the stairs ' method, then by placing the Romer on the map approaching the territory within the square from the south-west. Figure three of the six figure reference can then be read off one of the Romer's scales, figure six off the other, and the reference is pin-pointed exactly. Secondly, it helps a great deal to mark on each OS sheet, with mapping-ink preferably just in case rain happens to fall on the map and smudge all the ink, a periodic repeat set of bottom/top map figures, as well as those along the sides too. These should be written on the map in a standardised way, so there is no confusion as to which

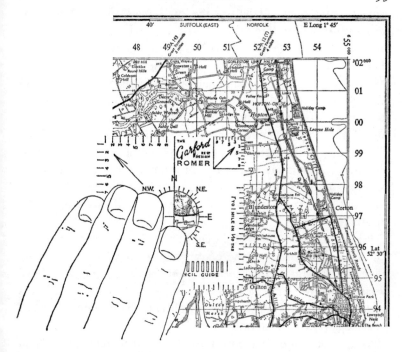

2 Here a Romer is shown in use on an Ordnance Survey one inch to the mile map. A reference is being plotted, using the Romer's scale offered up to the map in the time honoured fashion of 'Along the corridor—Up the stairs'. Mastering this simple procedure is the basis of British club rallying

square is being labelled by which figure. It is best to repeat these square location figures every ten kilometres, which means a navigator need not unfold his map to pick the figures off the extreme edges each time he needs to plot a reference. If part of a map has much intricate detail upon it, then it might be as well to refrain from adding to the confusion by inking in all the kilometre square numbers on this part of the map.

Virtually every club rally will require a navigator to have to plot references. After all, it is the only foolproof way of each crew putting an organiser's route on their own maps. It is often usual for all the references that are going to be required, to be issued to a navigator sometime before the start, so that he has time to plot them all before the car moves off, but there are still events where the route is only handed out, or rather the map references are handed out, actually as each car sets off. Then there is the occasional case where a route has to be dramatically changed due to an organiser finding that a road has become blocked for some reason or the other. Here route alteration references are pushed through the window actually along the route somewhere. So, every navigator should be prepared to plot a reference, at some time or other, actually on the move. This is far from easy for a number of all too obvious reasons; at the same time as having to plot, he might have to read out several junctions to his driver, as well as warning him of any nasty bends.

Having to look down at a map in a rally car, which might be jumping about all over the place, is an extremely good test of even the strongest constitution. Even the best navigators have been known to be car sick. Many navigators do take car sickness tablets, and it is certainly advisable to take along some 'Kwells', 'Sea Legs', or 'Marzine' just in case you do start to feel queasy. Many find that once they do begin to feel queer, then the only cure is to put the head back and turn the navigation light off. It is all very well doing this if a nice main road run is about to happen, but this is rarely the case. Some old hands subscribe to the view that once a navigator feels sick, the only cure is to be well and truly sick—safely out of the window of course! Perhaps the best advice for any novice navigator, is to take anti-car sickness tablets before the off, and, as with all pills, try them out first to ensure that no unpleasant side effects occur—it is possible for a wakey-wakey and an anti-car sickness pill to send the patient straight off to sleep. As with a driver, the right food ought to be consumed before a rally start, preferably avoiding excessively greasy or fancy dishes.

Take along enough pencils, so that time does not have to be spent on the event re-sharpening them. Pencils should not be too sharp, for they tend to break too easily and also go through the map. So that each rally's route markings can easily be erased, the grade of pencil must not be too hard. Most of the top navigators opt for 2B or 3B pencils. It is as well to take along a rubber, and a penknife, whilst the Romer should be secured around a navigator's neck with a piece of string.

There is always the tendency with all novice navigators to burden themselves down with cumbersome and over-complicated gadgetry. Map measuring wheels, stopwatch holders, average speed calculating disc computers, compasses—they are all really non-essential these days. A map board is necessary though, but this should not be too stiff, as this can prove to be very painful in a shunt. The best material for a navigator to use is hardboard, with the shiny side upwards. In an accident, this will fold up easily without causing obvious damage to a navigator's person. Thick wooden boards are out, as well as metal ones, whilst sheets of cardboard do not last out even one hectic night's motoring.

As with all the various marketed average speed devices, the impressive looking proprietary map boards are a complete waste of money.

The edge of a map board should be chamfered, so it does not prove too painful if it comes into violent contact with a driver's hand, which will be making frequent dives for the gearlever. Besides, apart from any consideration towards the driver, a navigator, has to realise that his valuable maps are extremely likely to become torn to shreds if they begin to flap too near the gearlever or handbrake. So the maps, plus board, should be kept away from the driver as far as possible. One worthwhile tip is for a set of rubber bands to be put around the map hardboard to keep them attached; especially useful if the navigator has to leap out of the car to help push it back on the road, and will want his maps to be in order on his return to duty. Some rubber bands round the sun visor are useful with which to secure square pencils. Pencils in pockets can be painful in an accident and anyway, they will stand a good chance of being broken by the safety belts, which should be worn by navigators at all times.

The responsibility for time is the navigator's. He should equip himself with a sturdy wrist watch, with a leather and buckle strap rather than a bracelet type, as these can all too easily release themselves during a rigorous night's rallying. It can then be set to rally time, or BBC time, whichever is going to be the most useful, of which more anon. A time piece will be essential to keep an eye on the overall time that any rally car is keeping, or not keeping, as the case may be. In addition a stopwatch is advisable if there are to be selective parts of the road section specially timed to the second, or special stages. Although the organisers will be recording the time taken on these sections, any navigator worth his salt should keep a check on their time, so he would also be advised to record the time taken in seconds. Carrying a stopwatch in a clip on the dash-board only clutters things up and usually annoys a driver by rattling, so perhaps the very best equipment for any navigator would be the purchase of a wrist watch, complete with a stop-watch section—but then the selection of Christmas present material is beyond the scope of this book.

MAPS

A navigator will quickly learn the real value of having his maps in first class condition. There are numerous systems in operation by the better navigators to store their maps, so that they can be picked out of a box in the back of the car easily. It is possible to compile a mammoth book, which would enable a navigator to simply turn pages to what would normally be another map, but simplicity in all things should be the maxim of every rallyist.

The best map equipment are the paper ones, purchasable either flat or folded. The flat ones can be folded into quarters though for speed of identification and ease of storage the paper folded variety are thought by most to be the best. You can purchase linen-backed OS maps, but these take up too much room stored, and are awkward to manoeuvre on the move. All maps must be kept in good condition; after a while it be-coming pointless to try to patch them up and new ones needing to be used. If a map is going to become an old chestnut for any navigator then he ought to line the folds on the reverse side with Sellotape as a temporary reinforcement. However when a new edition of a particular map is brought out, the old one should be replaced immediately. In the regulations of any event, the organisers will say which edition and which map numbers they advise navigators to use to follow the route. But when the time comes to put all the information on to a new map do not throw your old campaign map away. If ever a fire or flood swept through a rally car, as has been known, a navigator would have no duplicate information.

For long tracts of route on main roads, or when a rally changes part of the country, navigators find the quarter inch OS maps the most convenient, the overall picture of any club rally always being more easily gleaned.

It then helps in the marking up of your maps, to add to each edge the adjacent map number. Where an overlap occurs, the exact line of the overlap should be scribed on each map, so that a navigator knows when he can change maps if there is time. He can then change maps when the road becomes easier and he has time to do so, without leaving a switch of maps until he becomes involved directing his driver through a maze of junctions.

Many navigators have tried to build all sorts of complicated and ingenious map storage containers into their rally cars from time to time. On most club rallies, several maps are usually required, whilst, on the larger events, often shelves full have to be taken along. Their container should be flexible, light, and securely mounted or fixed in place. They should not be able to fall out due to a lively moment and must be out of the way of any water that may be flowing about a vehicle's floor. Above all, they should be easily identifiable from their stored position, as well as being accessible. As the navigator's seat often reclines, the best place for such a box, I have found, is behind the driver's seat, or if space permits, between the navigator's feet.

On the subject of stowing, it is wise to take along a waterproof document valise, not too bulky, to keep all the relevant paperwork intact. This should be sat upon or secured to a seat back with a bungee strap. If it is not instantly accessible, then the road book for checking into controls, should not be stored within. The route instructions will be more than likely in this road/route book as well, there being places vacant for the marshals to sign and/or stamp. There can in some cases be two separate documents—a time sheet and a road book. Maybe, once all the references are on the map, the road book can be stowed away, but the time sheet will still have to be kept on hand, so that time is not wasted hunting for it at controls or checks. One thing is certain, this booking-in sheet must be kept securely somewhere. There has been many a top rally crew put out of an event in the past by a spectator deciding to steal the valuable document as a souvenir, or then the navigator could drop it in the night, never to be seen again, on his way from the cockpit to lift some other car out of the way. Road books have also been lost before now, necessitating the unfortunate crew's retirement.

TIPS OF THE TRADE

As a navigator goes over the same territory more often, he will begin to know each map's idiosyncracies. Local knowledge is a very useful asset for any navigator to be able to impart to his driver, but it takes years to accumulate every peculiarity and bad bend on all the popular maps likely to be used on club rallies.

The short cut to the most well-known hazards and, more important, which track is passable and which is not, can be purchased in the form of a marked map. There are several enthusiastic navigators marking maps up these days. It is cheaper to buy rally maps from such amateur outfits, the locations of which can be ascertained from small ads in the enthusiast press, than learn all the ' goers ' and ' non-goers ' by laboriously trying to travel over them, and retiring from many rallies along the way awaiting the dawn and a pull out of the mud by a tractor. These map marker outfits either mark maps supplied by the navigator or supply brand new maps ready marked.

On most of the better rallies these days, the knowledge of whether a certain track is passable or not is not clearly as crucial as it used to be. There is normally sufficient time for all the map references to be plotted and all the queries about which way between the points the organisers intend competitors to use, to be cleared up.

The maximum overall average that organisers can legally inflict on road rallyists in the UK is 30 mph (though 50 mph is allowed for motorway sections), so therefore the distance between two controls cannot be more than half the number of minutes allowed for the section in miles.

The method organisers use to inform competing navigators which directions they are asking crews to approach and depart from controls is as follows. Before the reference, they put compass bearing directions, often trailing the reference with another direction. So, N 123789 SW would mean that the point at map reference 123789 should be approached from the north, with departure towards the south-west. Invariably, direction of departure is not mandatory, for if this is wrongly selected by a navigator leaving a control at a junction, the wrong direction of approach will occur at the next control point, or the competitor will waste time having to turn round on the wrong road.

There can be all manner of reasons for organisers demanding a specified direction of approach, the route may be too easy, shorter, near to many houses, or not allowed by the RAC (such points or squares are termed 'Black Spots'). Where the direction of approach is specified, then invariably there will be a penalty for any competitor who arrives at the control from the wrong direction. This will usually be as heavy as if he had missed the point altogether, so every care should be exercised to ensure that as much accuracy goes into the direction of approach/departure as in the plotting of the reference itself. It does not need much imagination to realise what could happen to two rally cars approaching each other down a narrow lane in the wilderness both really trying, and both assuming that they were on the correct route, and so, assuming it unlikely for anybody to be coming the other way. . . .

BLACK SPOTS AND MAP MARKING

Black Spots might appear to be all rather a bore. I cannot emphasise enough to newcomers the importance of their being observed for the very future of road rallying in this country. Areas or junctions have been declared 'Black' by the RAC

Motor Sport Division because there have been complaints from residents. By chancing a short cut, hoping nobody will have been posted to marshal ' Black Spot ' breakers, is only going to antagonise the locals further. In any case, rally routes are often so laid out, that any organiser should be able to spot instantly if a competitor has traversed an out-of-bounds area, by his suddenly appearing back in the rally further along the route back in time again. The penalty for being seen entering or coming out of an out-of-bounds area is nearly always exclusion. So navigators have been warned . . . displease not your driver by causing him to trespass in out-of-bounds areas.

The best marked maps will be capable of informing a crew on all manner of useful information, such as which tracks are not advisable if the weather is bad, traction in one or both directions becoming a problem. If ever a track is found by a really experienced navigator to have a very earthy surface as well as a steep gradient, he will then mark his map accordingly with an arrow to indicate that, although the track is passable, if the weather were to deteriorate then it would be impassable, or only a ' goer ', to rally cars in one direction. This would be then termed a ' wet down (or up) only goer '.

If a white road is impassable, then a navigator must make sure he adds a very clear cross onto his map. If the track does go, then he should tick it, or put a G for goer beside it.

The finer points of British club rally navigation can be extended to the marking by a navigator on to his map whenever a bend is ' not as map '. There are some notorious examples in Wales, where the road has been altered since the map has been compiled, or where the bend is more acute than it looks on the map. Often, a turn off a road may in fact be more of a hairpin and here a navigator would mark his map with a hairpin arrow, so that when the road is used complete with hairpin he can warn his driver in advance to be ready with the handbrake.

This same prior warning goes for which bits of road are rough or where there are particularly vicious humps in the road. In such cases the navigator should ink in to the side of the road on his map ' rough ' or ' hump '. Apart from being a very real advantage to a driver in a hurry, this sort of information helps to make rallying safer. Marking up maps is a vital part of crew preparation, and, while a driver labours away checking the car over, a good navigator should be working on his maps.

The best way to mark controls on the map is with ' C ', followed by its number, main controls ' MC ' and passage checks with ' PC '. The exact point should be arrowed with a V, with the point of the letter indicating the location. The route should all be corridored in pencil, with circles round the number, type of control, and its V. It is best if no pencil markings obliterate the roads constituting the intended route, as a vital junction might be obscured and valuable time lost.

Contour lines are on one inch to the mile maps, but you seldom see a novice ever using them, or ever really being aware of their existence. The gradient of the landscape is all charted by these lines, so any navigator has an instant spirit-level check of what the road he is directing his driver down actually should be doing as far as gradient goes. If snow conditions are very bad, then a thinking navigator will be able to forewarn his driver where difficulty in ascent is likely, or alternately how best the driver could avoid the worst inclines. It could be that a rally car is stricken near the end of an event with clutch slip and only by careful routing to avoid hills can a finish be achieved.

The actual height above sea level is printed into the contour lines at intervals along their length. The figure is printed so that when read they are facing uphill, a most useful ready check as to the direction of the slope. These lines are 50 feet of altitude apart and quite obviously, the closer the lines are together, the steeper the slope. A thinking wide-awake navigator would not direct a driver down a white road if it traverses contour lines that are very close together, that is if there is an alternative route round.

There are other features which are dependent on the weather too. Fords should all be marked, though lately most of the worst ones would appear to have been unsportingly filled in or bridged over. If it has been raining like cats and dogs for hours on end, it is well to consider an alternative route where a ford appears on the map across the intended route. Again, muddy sections can become impassable if the weather has been bad for days, so a top navigator will mark on his map ' impassable in wet weather ' where thick mud or floods are known by him to be a problem.

Taking map marking to a really fine art, then gates, as well as which way they open should be marked up with a small arrow. These days, gated roads, without marshals manning them, are used less often, but even so, attention to such detail might just prevent a driver from rounding a bend too quickly and cannoning into a gate that has blown shut. Also, a driver can pull up if necessary so that there is room for the gate to be opened. Then at the very top of the navigation tree, the best navigators will sometimes journey in a mid-week night to the remote parts of the country just to check out the severity of some bends, junctions and surfaces. But this is only when the rest of the particular team is right up to scratch, as well as the opposition becoming so powerful that such detailed dedication becomes necessary to win.

Landmarks are all marked on the map. It is most important and reassuring even if a navigator does not let his driver realise that he is chancing his rally car's direction to the stars, if the navigator can confirm that he has committed his driver to the correct road, when a stream, bridge, telephone kiosk or church luckily appears just where he hoped it would.

A navigator holds the reins to any rally driver, or should do. If there is an airfield along the route, and there often is, then he must prevent his driver rushing headlong into the wide open spaces. Most drivers love to open up their engines to the full on a rally whenever they can. They have perhaps been scurrying along in the lanes in the lower gears for most of the night when suddenly, they can pull maximum revs in top gear. It is all too easy if this is allowed to happen, to become hopelessly lost on the wide expanse of a derelict airfield. Finding the escape slot amongst the weeds and decayed perimeter buildings invariably needs the utmost care.

READING THE ROAD

Once knowing which is the right route, as well as beginning to develop the confidence of knowing that the car is being despatched by a navigator down the correct route, the next step is to progress from merely giving out the junctions, as well as including the other basic information. Naturally following the route on the map the same time as the car is covering it, can be made so much easier by reading the road. A navigator should start off doing this to himself always remembering to call up the junctions in good time. Reading the road in this way helps any navigator keep his place. Some navigators find they have to tilt the map towards them, so their quick glances at the road through the screen are less time consuming and more of a natural movement. The majority however seem to find it easier to feel where the car actually is from the ' G ' forces, only looking up to check that the junctions are in fact where they should be. Having directed their driver down the correct road, or slot in rally jargon, their head goes down again. One early mistake that any novice navigator makes is to call up the road at the expense of looking ahead for the junctions and control locations. Also once bend reading becomes an easier routine, and always if the driver actually finds an incessant chatter from his side preferable to sorting things out for himself, then really only the worst bends should be called up. Some drivers only really want to know the bad bends anyway, whilst others build up such a faith in their navigators that they start to drive purely on their navigator's reading, lining the car up for bends to the left and right as they are called before they even come into sight, and selecting gears for the grade of bend that is after the one that actually confronts them next. The reading of the road process needs to be built up gradually before a driver, being fair, should drive to purely what his navigator says. Expecting a novice to master road reading immediately is asking too much. The methods of grading bends seem to vary between fast, medium and slow, or bends can be called up in degrees. Which method is best is all a matter of personal preference. The choice of how the bends are called is usually in club rallies the prerogative of each navigator, whereas on Internationals, where pace note systems are equally as varied, the method to be used by a co-driver is dictated by a driver. When the road is called over to a driver, it can be helpful if the driver indicates to his navigator that he has heard each directional instruction, by saying 'Check'. Then, having completed the turn-off, fork or whatever, he can repeat the instruction, or say 'Done'. Often drivers tend to say 'Right', which can lead to obvious misunderstandings, even in the best organised cockpit. It is no use trying to use a driver as a store for directional instructions either; read ahead and keep him fully informed of the make-up of the next few sections by all means, but if too many instructions are dished out to most drivers at once, they forget them. They will then come back to their navigator in the middle of a complicated junction to ask them which way they should go. If a navigator had set about some calculation or using the restbit to maximum advantage, then both crew members are likely to land up lost. It will also become blatantly obvious to any navigator new to the sport that even the best drivers seem to mix their lefts with their rights. It is very helpful for a navigator to actually point down the slot that he intends his driver to take.

A navigator can pace a driver just by altering the speed of his road reading. This can be extremely helpful if a driver is beginning to lag in the early hours of the morning when there is no other rally traffic about to keep him awake. The only person, other than the penalties being dished out by the marshals, who can keep a check on any rally driver's performance is his navigator, his only audience. He should be able to tell, that is if he has not been lulled to sleep by ultra smooth driving, if his driver is slowing up. Encouragement and abuse can be employed on such occasions to keep the man of action at work.

Over-reading is a common fault of navigators too. By this, I mean when a navigator rushes ahead too much, his bend reading becomes pointless with the driver having to remember all that the navigator has said, as well as having to cope with what he sees directly ahead. But reading every twist and turn in fog can be a great help, not only for a crew to know exactly where they are, but also to keep the speed up. Some intelligent thought by the navigator can be helpful too, for if the fog proved to be consistently just on the low ground, he can speed

9 On the British Special Stage rallies, where often pace notes are forbidden, co-drivers, on the principle of four eyes being more accurate than two, should call out the bends and arrows as they see them. This is what Nigel Rockey's co-driver is doing in Ae forest on a Scottish. He is also demonstrating the effectiveness of a grab handle!

10 Everybody going rallying eventually runs out of road. Safety equipment should not be skimped, nor should the battle of trying to will the car back onto the road, during an accident ever be given up. Here Leo Bertorelli goes off, yet drives straight back onto the road again without applying the brakes, thus making a possible major incident a minor one.

11 Scrutineers are bound to look unkindly on any competitor's car that is presented to them in a filthy state. A clean and tidy looking car is invariably efficient, road worthy, and legally within Rally Regulations. Such is the case with Phil Cooper's ex-works 1293cc Cooper S.

12 Five, four, three, two, one—Go! Cars are usually released onto conventional Special Stages at minute intervals. Here, Phil Cooper, rather dirtier, waits the count down.

his driver up on the high bits, and the same in reverse if the mist were just on high ground.

The giving of plenty of information is a very important skill for any navigator. He must keep his driver fully informed of what is happening to the time, as well as how far he has to go to the next control. It is infuriating for any driver to have to drive in oblivion on a rally : not knowing how long he has in hand; how late he is; how many controls there are still to do; when the next official halt is; or whether he should save a great deal of time and money and turn round for home instead. This giving of information all helps to take a driver's mind off worrying about the office side of things completely. He can then concentrate on the driving and alter his pace accordingly. There is no earthly use in him hammering his car to bits, if there is plenty of time in hand. Conversely, there is no point in his dawdling along, only to run out of time, because through lack of information from his navigator, he did not know that the miles to do were beginning to outnumber the minutes left.

As well as the need for any driver to be able to flow his car along, a navigator should be part of his smoothness. His road reading should all contribute to this teams work, so that car, driver, and navigator work almost as one. There is sufficient conflict for these ingredients in the form of the elements, the route, and the time, without having navigation presenting any sort of a problem. If a long list of map references are thrust through a navigator's window, he should not immediately pull off the road to set about plotting them all because he would most probably find that he would run out of time at the very first control when his car eventually arrived. It is best for him to plot a couple of references only, forcing himself at least to try to plot ahead on the move. It is the only way to learn.

Another tip for a beginner is for him to be very much in charge of his driver, who, if he is a novice too, will be certain to be impetuous to have a go. It is much easier to drive instantly quickly rather than navigate. Every time another competitor rushes past, the novice driver will want to give chase. A navigator should try to prevent him doing this, for if he once loses the tow, by the marshals at the next control taking too

E

long in booking the car through for instance, they would find themselves completely lost. Then, of course, there is always the possibility of repeating somebody else's mistakes by blindly following them. It is always better for any crew to sort itself completely out before moving off down the road. The more a driver is allowed to rush headlong into the night, the further he is sure to go wrong. The navigator may not be able to even know where he is to start to direct a retracing operation.

A navigator should be the one who is expected to leap out of the car if necessary to check in at controls. More often than not, because of the almost universal acceptance of safety belts, the organisers will have arranged things on the administration side, so that he does not have to leave his seat, clock-ins being possible through the passenger window.

All instructions must be read by a navigator. This is vital in case something fundamental to the particular event's construction has been altered. Then the regulations must be read most carefully, the marking system being thoroughly understood. A copy should always be taken along by the number two.

Being able to see the map is an obvious necessity. I trust we can assume that a navigator will have found out whether he needs to wear spectacles or not before he ever considers reading maps on a rally. A map reading light is bound to have been fitted as standard rally equipment for any driver, but it is a wise precaution for a navigator to take along some back-up material too. This should be in the form of a spare bulb for the stalk light, as well as a torch map magnifier in case the main light source fails. If a torch device is to be used all the time, then spare bulbs and batteries should of course be carried. On the subject of map magnifiers, these are vital for a number of reasons. Firstly, this is the only sure way of reading a route's intricacies when a car is being thrown about. Secondly, the navigator using his own equipment can determine the brightness of the magnifier's illumination by a rheostat fitted as well. Thirdly, the absolute minimum of light will escape from a magnifier's shroud to distract the driver. For plotting several wide spread map references, a main map reading light will be necessary. But any driver will demand plenty of light shielding between the map reader's compartment and the screen to avoid the distraction of ghost images and glare. Even with one of the illuminated map magnifiers, this should be turned off if possible when not required to reduce light flickering out to the absolute minimum. The driver should provide the fixtures with his car preparation, the navigator the portable items.

CLOTHING

Unlike a driver, navigators should be prepared to have to put up with tramping around in the wet at controls, opening gates or trudging off into the night for help after retirement, whilst the driver catches up with his sleep. Sturdy boots or waterproof gum-boots are sensible. A navigator's feet are also more likely to become colder than a driver's, since they will be frozen to the floor for the most part. Drivers can at least keep their feet warm by operating the pedals with gusto. So double socks and warm waterproof boots are ideally required to be worn by navigators.

Some years ago every navigator was confronted with a Halda average speed indicator. Although these devices are most useful, their usefulness is now of little contemporary rally value. It is only on American events where ' Total Regularity ', meaning events run entirely on the marking of competitors achieving varying average speeds, that such a device has any real use.

These days a navigator can cope well enough with his map, Romer, pencil, map magnifier and main map light. It is helpful, if funds permit, to purchase a Halda or Gemini Trip measuring device, but I will deal with these in more detail when I cover cockpit preparation. Basically, one of these gadgets measures very accurately the miles covered in tenths, with the more expensive units having two measures, so that the total distance of the event can be clocked, as well as the broken down distance between junctions or sections. Usually such an instrument is mounted so the driver can glance at it as well. The advantage is obvious, for when a navigator tells his driver to proceed along a stretch of road for so many tenths of a mile unattended, he can then use the time with the driver on course, to work out or plot another reference. But the main help of a tripmeter is on the longer events, where the driver might have to go it alone whilst his co-driver sleeps, or where his co-driver merely reads off instructions identifiable with miles and tenths from a detailed road book. If different tyres are being used during an event, a set of gear wheels to alter the trip, so that it is accurate again, ought to be taken along. Ideally of course making the trip really accurate should all be tried out in test sessions before the rally.

AVERAGES

In practice, a rally car will always stand a very good chance of being late on interesting territory, so the average speed will not matter a great deal. But if the sections are easy, then a navigator must obey the ruling in force of the maximum average allowed, likely to be 40 mph. In most regulations, competitors will be penalised for being proved to have broken this maximum average speed between two points. It is an easy average to calculate anyway, it being one and a half minutes per mile.

If, on the first event, the newcomer hears some of the old hands muttering about ' Forty Checks ', they are referring to the possibility, or fact, of the organisers checking the average speed to catch competitors who exceed 40 mph. This is most usual on a main road run-in to a finish. Such checks are usually only instituted to satisfy the RAC Steward or the local police.

All sorts of methods of route marking can be used by organisers. On earlier rallies, some of these systems would be frowned upon by today's rallyist as being ludicrous. So tracings of bits of the route, cards with straight lines and branches off for all the various roads to the left and right of the intended route, a list of spot heights to go via, marked maps provided by the organisers, lists of map references in any order and optional sections looping off the main route are all becoming less common, though everyone seems to be faced with them at some time or the other.

TULIP

Of all the earlier methods used by organisers, the Tulip arrow, originated on the Tulip International, has lingered on. Indeed, most internationals use this method of laying their intended route out in competitors' road books. The idea with this Tulip system is that pictorial diagrams are used to indicate which way competitors should go at junctions. Distances are also shown alongside each pictorial instruction, both cumulative as well as the distance since the last diagram. In addition, signpost readings or specific features are put alongside the symbol.

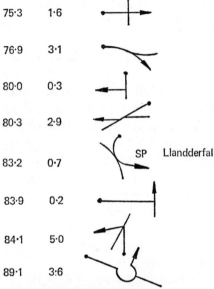

75·3	1·6	
76·9	3·1	
80·0	0·3	
80·3	2·9	
83·2	0·7	SP Llandderfal
83·9	0·2	
84·1	5·0	
89·1	3·6	

3 Here the 'Tulip' system of route instructions is shown. This would be the sort of thing the co-driver would have to follow in a major event's Road Book

TIMING

The timing of RAC approved events can be organised under two distinct systems; a time limit for the whole event, or a time schedule whereby a competitor is due at each control point at a scheduled time. Under these basic systems, there are various ways organisers are likely to implement timing.

The most usual method that competitors in British club events will encounter is the *Targa* system, named after the Oxford University Club's Welsh classic road event, the Targa

Rusticana, from which the timing system stemmed. By *Targa,* it is meant that the first car, if it were on time, would be due at each control at the same time, the marshals' watches all having been set back to accommodate the number of minutes allowed by the organisers for a car to travel over each section between the controls without losing any time. So, car number one will, if on time, arrive at each control at the same time on the watches—oo-oı hrs in fact. If a clock reads oo-o8 hrs, then he will have lost seven minutes along the way somewhere, so will have the appropriate number of penalty points accordingly. Car number two will be due at each control at oo-o2 hrs, car number three at oo-o3 hrs, and so forth. All the clocks are set by the Clerk of the Course in advance, before the marshals set off to their various control points, as well as being finally checked when he opens the route just before the competitors are due to arrive. The timing on all the clocks must tie up with the official limit of a 30 mph overall average speed.

It can be that the competitor will be faced with a system where ' BBC Time ' is quoted for each control, with either the number of the car already added, one car each minute, in the road book, or this may be left to the competitor to work out for himself. This is the timing used on the RAC's own RAC Rally of Great Britain for instance.

The third and least used method of rally timing is that of ' Regularity '. Here an average is prescribed by the organisers. This has to be achieved by a competitor at all times or varied if the average is altered along the route. Organisers mark competitors on ' Regularity ' timed events by laying on secret, undisclosed, on-sight controls, along the prescribed route as handed out to competitors at the start control.

A really accurate illuminated dash-mounted clock of the type used by the RAF is best for checking the time by both the crew. But this should preferably be detached when the crew are not occupying the cockpit, as these clocks always seem to be highly prized by looters who descend on any abandoned rally car. The best sorts of clocks, although expensive, are twin ones, so that the overall time can be seen, as well as the time elapsed on a particular section or stage. If the competitor does not want to go to the trouble of purchasing special timing equipment, then, of course, a decent sized robust wrist watch will suffice.

The methods of timing vary from rally to rally, but whatever the system used, it is the navigator who should make himself responsible for checking that the time given to his crew by the marshal is the correct one. If this is done by a stamp-out printing clock, then there can hardly be any argument, but even so, the ink must be checked for legibility. If the time is written down by a marshal from a master clock, then the navigator should make it his business to check that the time on the clock is indeed the time that has been written down on his documents. It is all too easy for a mistake to be made under pressure, especially if it is raining, and a great many cars are screaching into the particular control point at the same time. If an alteration is necessary ever, it is vital to ensure that the marshal in charge verifies the alteration by signing alongside it.

Many rallies used to use the ' sealed watch ' method of timing. Either the navigator's own watch was sealed into a small clear plastic box, or the organisers provided a set of sealed pocket watches usually in return for a refundable deposit. These watches were all set a minute different, so that with cars all starting off along a route at one minute intervals each car was due at each control at the same time on each watch. With this method, a navigator could have quite an advantage if he were to call up the time he wanted rather than the time actually on the watch in his hand. Sharp eyed marshals would never let any navigator get away with this one. But even the best navigator might try it regardless of the system used, especially if he knows he is in fact late. This may appear to be dishonest. It is. But he who allows the others to have the benefit of cashing in on this potential advantage, has not learned yet another wile of rallymanship.

The Co-Driver

The logical progression from reading off the bends and hazards from OS maps is the compilation of pace notes for special sections, where practice is possible. This difficult technique, as well as the more general use of the Tulip road book, instead of a list of map references, is all more of a co-driver's lot.

A club rally navigator would have to pick up these specialised co-driver's skills, if he were to go rallying abroad, or if he were to hope to tackle our home internationals. Of course, most club rally navigators' skills apply for co-drivers too. But there are additional requirements, necessary for the longer events.

Often navigators imagine that a co-driver's streets are paved with gold. Perhaps for the top few in the works teams this might appear to be so. But, if the truth were known, the apparent opulence, with the best hotels and jetting everywhere, is only possible thanks to expenses. The top co-drivers earn very little compared to the drivers, whose retainers are more on a par with the professional racing driver.

Unlike a navigator, whose main job is keeping the car on the right road, a co-driver's function in the rally world is to be at all times master of the paperwork, often voluminous on an international.

If a career is envisaged out of being a rally co-driver forget it. The job is very short-lived even for those who do make a works team. It is also extremely difficult to try to combine being a co-driver on the larger (and therefore longer) events, as well as keeping some sort of a steady job when so rarely at home. Once the more important events are undertaken, the amount of time off work will quickly eliminate the problem. An employer is better off without having a rally co-driver on his staff. Anyway in a final desperate attempt to put the outsider off the idea, living out of a suitcase for weeks on end is not as much fun as it might at first seem. Being a co-driver is hardly training for any other job afterwards.

There are many first-class co-drivers about who might find it all rather a strain if they were dumped into a rally car at the start of a Welsh restricted rally. The navigation facing the co-driver as opposed to navigator, even on the toughest European rally, is rarely involved. If the right preparation ground work has been done, there will be no ' Hunt the slot '.

The co-driver will be expected to drive on the event and on the longer events, he may have to drive well over half the

13 The Author powerboating in the Hafren Forest on the 1968 Gulf London International Rally, using the same Mini Cooper S in which he finished a dozen Internationals.

14 Daylight Special Stage events over interesting tracks on private property, closed to other traffic, are rapidly becoming the most important training ground for private owners. Here, the emphasis is on driver ability and car preparation, more than navigational skill.

15 At least with rallying, a competitor can use anything. Here, the Harkness/Bannister Fiat 850S sees some fine scenery on an International Rally, namely the Circuit of Ireland, yet at the same time remaining a perfectly tractable road car.

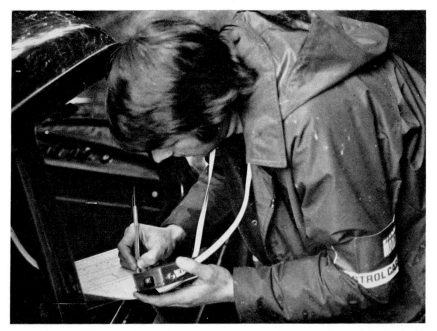

16   Competitors must ensure that the Marshal legibly fills in his Control Point's details in the right places on the official documentation. It is up to a crew to check that the time written down is the one on the clock.

17   For safety, and to give competitors sufficient room to slow down progressively, the ends of most Special Stages have ' Flying Finish ' points. Here, a popular clubman's rally car, an Escort GT, driven by Roger Platt, completes the Tor Head Stage over closed public roads on the 1970 Circuit of Ireland.

18 Some rallies use printing clocks from Longines. A Co-dri:er should make sure that his time card is correctly inserted so that the time is stamped in the right place. It does pay off for him to wait by the clock for the exact minute he requires to come up. Also, before leaping back into his rally car, he should be sure that the clock has in fact stamped the time legibly.

distance, whilst the driver sleeps. The co-driver is often expected to be somewhat of a Superman, who is expected to be able to do without sleep altogether. Well, this is what the average driver seems to expect. The best rally drivers even, leave all the talking to their co-drivers. The co-driver is supposed to know every foreign language fluently, regardless of which country the particular rally is passing through. It is quite amazing how it is the co-driver who is left by his driver to explain away the driver's speeding offences to a posse of sinister Gendarmes. On this language front, French is definitely the most useful second language for any co-driver. The regulations for any international rally are bound to be printed French. Also, it does not seem to matter in which country the co-driver finds himself, some basic knowledge of French might well be known by the locals, where English is found totally incomprehensible.

READING THE REGULATIONS

In view of some of the controversy that has arisen on internationals in recent years, with whole teams, as on the Monte, being disqualified, reading—and understanding—the regulations is vital for any co-driver. There is no point in setting off on an international, with the ever-increasing costs, unless the regulations have been absolutely mastered by the co-driver. It is again the co-driver who must make it his job to read up the regulations in the evenings prior to a rally start, whilst his driver relaxes.

Further to having a deep working knowledge of the regulations for each event entered, the co-driver should also take with him a copy of the FIA's rules governing rallying. In the unfortunate event of a dispute at the end of a rally, as is regrettably so often the case, again it is the co-driver who is expected to be able to enhance, defend, or represent his driver's case for less penalties in front of the stewards. Being a convincing orator is an excellent quality for the budding co-driver. Indeed, some of the best co-drivers in the business would perhaps do well as barristers. They have in many cases had plenty of practice.

A thorough familiarity of the regulations cannot be

emphasised enough. The method of marking for the event being tackled must be learned off pat. During a rally, the co-driver might have to make split-second decision of policy, so he must know exactly what sort of effect any of his decisions may have on the position of his car in relation to the outcome of the results. Unless he knows the regulations, he will be unable to direct the pace of his driver, for he will not understand the timing of the event. One of the fundamental rules of conduct for any rally crew is to know at all times just how slow to go to win. Unless the driver is told by his co-driver, he is more likely to keep breaking the car through pointless over-driving, rather than winning. Win or finish, the fate of every rally car is as much in the hands of the co-driver as the driver. It is a wise driver who realises this.

If the rally being undertaken by a crew is a special stage event in Great Britain, then the roads or tracks used by the organisers will be on private property and, because practice is for the most part forbidden on British rallies, these stages will be unseen prior to the event by the crew. But, if practice is permitted on even part of these sections, or all, as on most Continental events, then a crew is unlikely to do well if it does not take advantage of this.

RECCE

The advantage of prior knowledge of what happens to the road over each and every brow is obvious. Anybody would only have to prove this conclusively for himself by driving as fast as he could from point A to point B, taking the road as unseen. Then after driving over the road several times, his earlier time would be decimated, if he had not flown off the road through over-confidence. So, if it is possible to go over all the route before a rally, at least the co-driver should do so. Such an exercise is termed a recce, often very time consuming but, if at all possible financially or within the time available, a recce should be carried out.

As with the event itself, a recce should be planned most carefully. There will usually only be so much time and money available. These ingredients must be used frugally. If time is really tight, the co-driver should just take a look at the parts of the route that might give him trouble navigationally on the event itself. The route will be known in advance by competitors on all the leading continental events. The sections that will matter are the specially timed ones, as well as cities, which often can be very confusing to traverse first time. Ideally, enough time should be made available for all the road sections, as well as the special sections, to be carefully looked at with a view to the co-driver making two sets of notes; firstly navigational notes, and secondly pace notes.

The methods of carrying out this note-making operation are legion. Often the co-driver has to carry out the initial recce alone, so a tape recorder and the tripmeter can be the most practical combination. This way, the co-driver does not have to stop in hotels for a mammoth transfer session from tape to written word quite so frequently. The traditional ballpoint and note book is perhaps the most reliable system, although, on a long event this can be rather a clerical chore. Invariably, reams of notes scribbled down in a moving car will need taking down all over again in more legible form. But then if the co-driver is on his own, having to drive and navigate himself around his recce, the tape recorder is the only feasible way of completing the job in reasonable time. If this has to be the case, in the interests of accuracy he should personally transcribe his tapes, or at least check the typing afterwards by carefully listening to them. The destiny of himself, driver and rally car, through their accuracy, must be considered to be at stake. As far as possible, the route of the rally on the recce should be covered by the co-driver at exactly the same time of day as the rally goes through the territory. This will give him a much clearer assimilation of exactly what the conditions will be like on the event itself, not only as far as the visibility goes, but also for a guide to traffic density. If roads are going to have to be taken flat out by a driver on an event, it is as well to be able to know whether he should expect roads to be clear of lorries, or whether he should be prepared for any hazard from hordes of them in the middle of their daily routine to some quarry along the route. A set of hairpins might seem fine on a recce in the middle of the night, but a fleet of school buses taking up most of the road on the event itself might prove to be an all too expensive hazard. Towns, speedily crossed in the night, can really delay a rally car in a hurry during the day, especially if the timing coincides with a local rush-hour.

200			START 5^H EPPEUVE			
7·2	7·2	!	FORK R	SP	POIDS LOURDS	(R.F.)
8·4	1·2		FORK L	NO	SP	
14·9	6·5		FORK R	SP	COL DE ROUSSET	076
26·0	11·1		FORK L	SP	VASSIEUX	
32·0	6·0	!	L AT T	SP	LA CHAPELLE	0178
38·7	6·7		FINISH EPREUVE + KEEP R.SP LA CHAPELLE			
40·6	1·9		LA CHAPELLE			
41·2	0·6		R AT T	SP	DIE	N518
41·45	0·25		FORK L AT ELF, GENDARMERIE ON R			
42·5	1·15		KEEP L			

4 These navigation notes indicate the sort of information that a factory co-driver would expect to find his way by on the road sections linking special tests. Such notes would be prepared on the recce, the sample being taken from the ones checked by the author for the Ford Team on the 1970 Monte Carlo Rally

As well as trying to carry out the recce at roughly the same time of day or night as the rally, some idea of the sort of time a crew may expect to take to cover the route is very important. Throughout a recce, a co-driver must log running time, obviously discounting any meal or sight-seeing stops along the way. The times must also be broken down further for each individual part of the route. More often than not, it will be found that a time a co-driver thought was pretty unrealistic over a certain stretch of route will turn out to be easily on when it comes to the event itself. There is nothing like the real thing to make even the meekest personality put the bit between his teeth.

Often a co-driver might be doing a recce on behalf of several crews, who might not have the time themselves to be able to carry out their own recce, perhaps to confine their limited look-see to the special sections. So the weather conditions and times must be simulated as far as possible by he who actually carries out the communal recce for a team or group of individuals. Even with works teams, on the longer events especially, the budget available may prevent each works crew from doing a full recce. So one co-driver will be despatched first to cover the route for the overall navigational recce, to be followed up by a driver going along as well to assist at more like rally speeds, so that the pace notes for the special sections can be compiled.

Particularly in mountainous country, the time of day a piece of road is travelled along can make quite a difference to the road conditions. The trickling of a mountain stream across a road, doing nothing more than making a slightly damp patch on the surface in the afternoon sunlight, can change dramatically in the early hours of the morning to a slick of treacherous ice. If at midday, a twisty little track alongside a stream for the length of a valley does not prove to be much of a problem to a recce crew, swirling nocturnal mist when the rally passes can alter enormously a forecast of the sort of time that the crew was expecting to clock-up.

The newcomer to making notes may fall into the trap of over-complicating them. They must be as simple as possible and, to alleviate the chore as much as possible, a set of standardised abbreviations must be worked out and followed assiduously. These will save time and, by their more certain legibility, will make the transcription job so much easier back home. If the recce is a last minute rushed job, as might sometimes have to be the case, and copies have to be made at the same time as the original set of notes is being compiled, then carbon paper will be required and neatness become even more vital.

Where the notes are going to be passed on to the others by the co-driver, the time taken perhaps can be expressed in various gradings. A colour coding of the various sections is all very artistic, but never as effective as a percentage of marking out of ten. When a driver hears a section requires eight tenths driving effort, and it is followed by one that calls for a speed up to ten tenths, he is more likely to know what he is supposed to do with his right foot than if he were simply told blue to

green, with a touch of red thrown in. Apart from the degree of
driver effort required in a graded system, a co-driver on his
recce must grade the surface too—a factor he should take into
consideration anyway when deciding on what amount of an
overall effort is to be required from his driver. Something on
the lines of tarmac, gravel, dirt, mud, rocks or potholes should
suffice, although for winter rallies the presence of thick or
patchy snow, or ice must not be forgotten either.

   Throughout a recce a co-driver will be logging distances, both
cumulative as well as for each section, and, in the more advanced forms of note-taking, distances will be broken down
between junctions and bends. The only way to do this accurately
is to use a proper trip device, which might prove on occasions
to be a problem if a hired car is used. The best organised rally
crew will have a replica to their actual rally vehicle specially
for recce work. A better indication of how the real car will fare
on the event itself will result for a start. Such a practice car
will more than likely be equipped with the same sort of tripmeter as the rally car, so the distances logged will be one
hundred per cent accurate and will tie up on the rally with the
distances from the recce notes.

   So the driver can have as much time to get used to a co-
driver's driving as possible prior to the rally itself, a co-driver
should be allowed to drive the driver as much as possible on the
recce. It is quite normal for any driver to be a dreadful
passenger. A co-driver must break the driver's habit of nail
biting himself to pieces by attempting to instill confidence,
and the best way to condition any driver to his partner being
let loose in the driving seat is to allow him plenty of wheel
time. Then, before the event proper, the split up of the driving
must all be pre-decided. The co-driver should drive anywhere
on the route where it might be possible for the driver to get
some rest, but he should only drive to rest the number one
driver for the tests or parts of the route which were discovered
on the recce as likely to be tight on time.

   The novice co-driver might have been rallying before as a
navigator on club events, or even driven his own car. Invariably,
the major fault with the beginner to the co-driver's seat is that

he often imagines he has to drive as fast as the number one driver. His only contribution to the driving of a rally car is to give the main driver a rest. His driving should more than anything else be safe. He should strive to conserve the car as much as possible, so that the car and number one can be stored up for the sections that are known in advance to be what will matter. A co-driver's driving should be smooth rather than spectacular. It is the smoothness which should be impressive.

PACE NOTES

There are purists who have decried the almost universal adoption of pace notes in the big league of international rallying. They would prefer that all rallies should be run entirely over unseen roads. This would certainly help to keep costs down, as it would eliminate the expensive performance of a recce. I would agree that it is certainly unfair on events where the differentiation in performance between the factory teams and the rank and file is accentuated unduly by the factory cars having notes, whilst the privateers have to cope with the road as it is seen by them actually on the rally for the first time but, when all have access to make notes, then it is at least equality again, albeit at a more advanced level. Pace notes, well rehearsed, make for faster rallying. They make the sport considerably safer too. Surprisingly though, it is possible for a crew to put up a slower time over a section by taking the reliance of such notes too far, the wild abandon of the driver being tamed by what are in effect a set of instructions.

Putting aside inaccuracies, pace notes must also be completely devoid of ambiguity. This can occur in the most simple way. For instance, if a driver were to confuse his co-driver's shouting 'Right' for 'Slight', the car could land up off the road for good through the driver taking a definite bend too fast. But then, as the safety of both driver and co-driver depend on the notes being heard and understood clearly, there are unlikely to be repeat mistakes.

If the time is available during the recce, several runs over the special tests should be attempted. Initially, a fairly brisk run should be made so that the feel of the test is understood, while at the same time any navigational notes should be made, together with the distances between junctions. Next, after an about turn, or preferably, if possible, trying another route round back to the start of the test again to avoid being clobbered by another competitor out practising at rally speeds, a really detailed note-taking run should be made. It is best to use a fairly ample note book for this, rather than separate sheets of paper, as there is less chance of a page becoming detached from its correct order, to be destroyed underfoot on the floor, necessitating a repeat of the whole test all over again to be sure that all the notes are in the same order as the bends themselves. Plenty of space should be allowed between each symbol for subsequent alteration, the best scribing implement being a felt-tipped pen, the broad strokes of which do not smudge and can be clearly seen in a dimly illuminated cockpit in motion.

Often the initial note making is done by the co-driver on his own, so it is then up to the driver to run over the test at about eight tenths of his maxim—quick enough to tell whether the notes swing or not. As he completes this run, repeated again and again by the star rally drivers over several weeks, he upgrades the notes according to a combination of the car, as well as the conditions likely to be encountered. The co-driver should either change the marking grade altogether, or merely add a plus for faster and a minus for slower above each symbol. It must also be understood that, although a set of comprehensive notes may do in the main for successive occasions, the best pace notes are especially right for a certain car in certain weather conditions. Each driver will view a particular bend differently in a different car. When I helped behind the scenes to mark up pace notes for the Ford team on a Monte I was very soon aware of the difference between each team driver's notes, or rather his interpretation of how he would like the road read over to him.

So in basic form, pace notes describe the road, where either memorising it becomes impossible, or for any driver who has never seen the test before. In advanced works driver form, they describe to him how fast he can take his car over the roads at the actual time of the rally.

19 Extremes of the elements are all part of the sport's challenge. Rain, floods, or fords may have to be tackled. Any rally engine's waterproofing must be foolproof if stalling in the middle is to be avoided. Here Paddy Hopkirk and Tony Nash, nice and dry in the comfortable interior of their Triumph 2.5 PI, go for a dip.

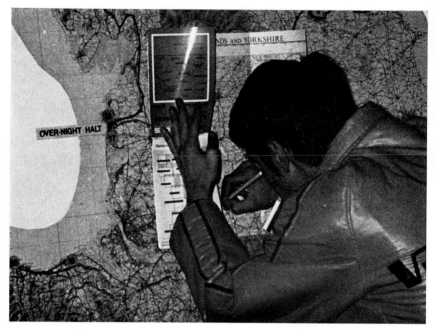

20 There may be opportunities when the route details are handed out at the start itself, for navigators to check or copy their route from a master one displayed by the organisers at the start HQ. Queries should be resolved at this time rather than when the event is under way.

21 Even on the smallest club event, a crew will be confronted with a mass of paperwork. The more events attempted, the less the confusion. Crews should however always read every word most carefully.

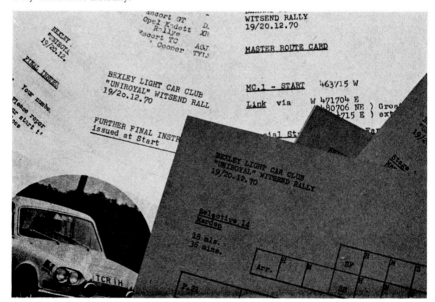

Reading pace notes for the first time will quickly dispel any brash confidence in the novice that it is all rather simple. A great deal of practice at compilation, understanding all the problems involved, and reading them is really required. The timing and delivery of pace notes to a driver can make a very significant difference to the sort of time he puts up. The reading must not be too fast, nor too slow. The driver should never be expected to remember too many instructions at once, but at the same time he must be given some indication as to what the road is likely to do the bend after next on a slow piece of road, and the bend after the bend after next if the going is fast. The speed of the note reading has to be varied throughout. The only way a co-driver can do this is to feel the car and tune in the notes with what has to come next, as long as no symbols are missed out in error. There is no room for error in pace note reading. The whereabouts at any one time cannot be re-discovered by the co-driver looking up to work out where he has reached. There will only be time for the quickest glance occasionally, just to make sure that landmarks are appearing where they should be in the notes. On some sections whole stretches are very similar with left and right bends all being about the same radius for mile after mile; a co-driver on such occasions will do well to litter his pace notes with kilometre stones if they are going to be visible above the snow, signposts, ringed telegraph poles and other geographia. It is quite amazing what an effect is has on a hesitant driver, if a co-driver slips in a ' hairpin right after a parapet ' just before it hoves into view. Regular confidence boosts in this way make for fast times, though no driver will want his notes being too freely cluttered up with trivia. Pace notes must be simple, or else it becomes too difficult in the time available in a modern rally car between turns for a driver to speedily translate the instructions he receives from his co-driver into how he should drive from the notes.

There is another most useful use for landmarks in pace notes. If a driver has a spin or incident and the co-driver loses his place in the notes during the melée, then regaining the notes will be that much more possible. Besides, a driver will need the notes more than ever to catch up all the lost time.

F

All sorts of different symbols have been used for the same set of alternatives. Most of these are variations on a theme. The ones that I think are the clearest, easiest to read and understand are as follows:

HPR	hairpin right
OHPR	open hairpin right
MR	medium right
FR	fast right
VFR	very fast right
Ř	flat right
HPL	hairpin left
OHPL	open hairpin left
ML	medium left
FL	fast left
VFL	very fast left
Ľ	flat left

Then in addition TIGHTENS can be introduced after a symbol, whilst LONG can precede if relevant. If a bend is more acute than its symbol suggests, but not tight enough for the next grade of symbol, then MINUS can be added. So, for instance a L MINUS is tighter than an ordinary left, but less acute than a hairpin left.

To help the co-driver read pace notes fluently, it can be useful to link the symbols together with + or AND. But the real benefit of linking symbols together is to do this selectively, so that, when bends are consistently continuous, they are linked with ANDS. When there is a gap in their frequency, a pause in the script can be put into the notes with a blank space between the set of symbols and the next distinct item. If one bend leads into another this can be put over in the notes by an arrow pointing to the next symbol. Idiosyncracies such as KINKS, TUNNEL or BRIDGE are most helpful too. Where there is any doubt about the finality of a symbol, then the notes should have a ? behind it. If extra special attention is needed, the word CARE can be slotted in either before or after a symbol. Because there is a difference between FLAT or FAST, it is best to add a Saint-type halo above the direction of the bend for FLAT, which really does mean all systems go for any driver. Where there is a straight piece of road, usually fairly brief on a rally special section, the notes should have the straight categorised in units, such as 50, or 100 etc. Such figures need not necessarily mean yards, but must be consistent throughout a set of notes so the driver knows the sort of length of each straight for maximum acceleration he may expect.

The pace notes should be well labelled up for each test, so that there is no possibility of the wrong notes being picked up for the wrong section, as sometimes the same test is used from opposite directions on the same event. Pace notes should also tie in exactly with the navigation notes for the road linking sections. The following example from the classic Monte Carlo Rally *Turini* mountain test may prove useful. (What the navigator would say is beneath each line.)

Turini: Moulinet—La Bollene
Notes start from Hotel de la Post:

HPR	300	LONG ML	50

Hairpin right / Straight 300 / long medium left / straight 50 /

LONG L̊	50	HPR	50

long flat left / straight 50 / hairpin right / straight 50 /

R̊	100	LONG FL AND VFL AND L̊	

flat right / straight 100 / long fast left and very fast left and

	50	LONG FL AND FL TIGHTENS AND	

flat left / straight 50 / long fast left and fast left tightens and

LONG R MINUS	50	L̊ AND VFL AND	

long right minus / straight 50 / flat left and very fast left and

LONG R̊ ?		100	R̊

long flat right—not quite / straight 100 / flat right /

100	LONG VFL TIGHTENS → FL AND	

straight 100 / long very fast left tightens into fast left and flat

Ł AND   Ř → VFR   KINK   50
left and flat right into very fast right / kink / straight 50 /

            VFR AND Ł   100   FL
very fast right and flat left / straight 100 / fast left /

      50
straight 50, etc.

ICE NOTES

On a winter classic like the Monte, the conventional pace note
can be taken one stage further—the ice note. Most of the leading teams run a complete duplicate set of Ice Note crews
behind the scenes during Monte week. Each ice note crew is
assigned to some of the special sections by each team. The idea
is for them to mark up the pace notes belonging to that team
with accurate up-to-the-minute surface conditions. Because of
the detailed work involved and the need for copying the ice
and snow information onto all the team cars' notes, one single
ice note crew will not suffice per works car. If such a crew did
exist, then they would be quick enough to be able to win the
rally themselves.

Again referring to my experience with Ford, under the
direction of Stuart Turner, the very best method of marking up
notes is to use two colours. Felt-tip pens are best for this
purpose, red for ice or snow, and blue for water. Variations
in ice/snow or water/damp can be shown under each instruction in the pace notes by using a solid to dotted line.

As often it is virtually impossible to compile detailed surface
notes in the minutes leading up to when the rally cars set off
on the stage, because the authorities close the roads off, a very
good plan is to cover the sections twenty-four hours before the
rally. Then the ultimate information can be obtained by plant-
ing ground thermometers on the highest points of each section,
so that, just before the event, the ice note crew, leaving themselves sufficient time to be able to return to the start of the
section again, can check whether the temperatures are above
or below those they discovered during the detailed run the day

before. On the final brisk run over the section, the ice notes crew can then amend any of their markings which might no longer apply due to the most recent weather changes.

The Ford team go one stage further still, by also transferring the colour markings from the notes on to a summary aerial-view sketch of the section, so that, whilst the co-driver is quickly flicking through the ice/water markings on his pace notes, the driver can gain an overall forecast impression of what to expect. At this point, before setting off he can then select exactly the right type of tyre for the conditions he is about to encounter. The co-driver will also have found out from the service and ice note crew what sort of tyre the opposition, who may have started the section before them, used.

WHEN NO NOTES

However, on events where there is no chance of any pace notes, the co-driver should not sit like the proverbial sack of potatoes on the stages, whilst the driver is at work. Events where roof lights are still allowed, then the co-driver at least can assist in providing light for the driver when the main lights have sunk into a hollow or are shining the wrong way into the trees for the corner ahead. But unfortunately, roof lights have been virtually outlawed on the roads of Europe these days. A co-driver can still however shout out the severity of a bend when his driver, because of the fall of that bend in relation to the side of the car in which he happens to be sitting, cannot see round. The same applies, particularly on public roads, when for the most rapid progress all the road ideally needs to be used. This may be very necessary if a crew is late or, being on the continent, the driver is sitting on the wrong side of the car for safely seeing to overtake a bulky vehicle. Even on forestry special sections, it is no bad thing for any co-driver to shout out the direction of the arrows, when he catches sight of them. Often because of the very nature of a loose undulating forestry track with a rally car being for the most part in the air, a driver might become so absorbed steering his bucking steed between the trees that he might miss vital arrows at a junction. So, following the principle that four eyes see better than two, a co-driver should not sit out arrowed stages in silence—unless of course the driver prefers it that way.

Another very important point for all co-drivers to bear in mind is when a driver finishes a stage, he must be told immediately which way to go at the next junction. So often a rally car rockets over a stage finishing-line, only to sit there steaming, whilst the co-driver collects himself together, sorts out his maps, drops most of the paperwork in the mud, and finally allows the driver to impetuously roar off in entirely the wrong direction. A good co-driver will have it all worked out before the car ever reaches the end of the special section, so no road time is wasted. On the other hand, a driver will not be very flattered if, in the middle of a particularly hectic stage, his co-driver decides to work out where they will in fact be when they come out of it onto the public road again. The rustle of paper and the flicker of a navigation light at such a time can become infuriatingly distracting to any driver, who is attempting to take his job seriously.

FUEL AND SERVICE PLANNING

It is the co-driver's job to find out on a recce the accurate availability of fuel supplies. He must naturally find out whether such supply sources are open at the time the rally is due to pass and it might be as well, while doing this job, to make a thorough job of it by making a note of the facilities at the garage, such as the availability of welding equipment and so forth, the opening times, the telephone number, and the proprietor's name.

Where the weight of the rally car may become crucial on the special sections, knowing just how low a driver can allow his rally car's fuel to run might be very important. Not only does the exact location of more fuel and its availability become, in such cases, of prime importance to a crew, but also the car's fuel consumption, especially when being pushed to the limit, must be most carefully calculated by the co-driver before the rally starts. He should then be able to tell the driver precisely when and where to take on fuel, and indeed how much as well. Where two almost identical cars tackle the same stage, with the same weather conditions, then the importance of being able to start (and what is more important finish) with as light a weight of fuel on board as possible is basic strategy.

In addition to the fuel plan being worked into the navigation notes, the competent co-driver should also work in all the appropriate manufacturers' service points. On the more important events, all the component firms will most probably field service vehicles. So tyre, brake, oil and electrical service availability should be added to the navigation notes. Where a vehicle manufacturer is putting out its own service crews, they usually only want to know about their own works cars. The private co-driver should therefore concentrate on discovering the positioning around the route of the Customer Tuning Departments, often specially fielded to look after private owners—an obvious example is British Leyland Special Tuning. If the event is a less important one, with only the crew's own service crew being in attendance, the co-driver should still know at all times where to expect service. It might just be possible to keep a car in a rally if a link-up with a service point goes smoothly.

It is all very well a co-driver knowing how much time there is available to fix the car if it goes wrong, but it would all be rather a waste of effort if the exact location of the required service assistance is not known. Planning of the service points even in the most amateur rally team is another responsibility of the co-driver. On the larger events, all the various firms that are servicing their customers' equipment usually hand out cards with the whereabouts of their own specialised service points if assistance might be required. Rather than carry all these pieces of paper along, the well organised co-driver should transfer all the various service points onto his navigation notes, avoiding the potential confusion of being cluttered up with unnecessary impedimenta.

On the event itself, it is the co-driver who must know exactly how long there is available on any occasion for those at the service points to work on the car. In his planning, he should organise the service so that it is positioned where it is most likely to be needed, after a particularly hectic section for instance, as long as there is a likelihood of there being time available to do any work on the car. If it is certain that there will be time to spare, then a routine service should be planned. The same goes for making the most of the time in hand when a meal stop for the crew is predicted. The co-driver should plan for a service crew to be positioned for work whilst the crew are eating—never a popular directive with service crews.

THIS AND THAT—BUT ORGANISED

The co-driver should do all the booking of hotel rooms before, during, and after the longer events. Even if there is only an hour or so available, then the co-driver should see to it that his driver is directed to a hotel room for some shut-eye. There are apparently some super-human drivers and co-drivers who can do without sleep, but the vogue amongst today's top rally competitors is for as much sleep as is possible on an event. The co-driver should of course first ensure that a really reliable wake-up call is arranged with the hotel staff, tipping heavily if there is the slightest possibility of anybody allowing a co-driver or driver to over-sleep. Even some of the most important rally crews in the business have overslept in the past, so having to set off on the following sections late. Perhaps the well-equipped co-driver should take along with him an alarm-clock: apart from sponge bag, towel, toothbrush and paste, as well as some toilet paper. Thus equipped, he would at least be ready for anything. Otherwise, the same clothing tips already discussed for drivers apply.

Although a particular event may be extremely well documented with a road book that might appear to the co-driver as being so comprehensive that his maps would be superfluous, the all-thinking co-driver will never be lulled into a foolish state of total reliance on this. Maps should always be taken along, regardless of the detail of the organisers' route guidance paperwork and, where possible, in cases where the route is given out in advance of the start, a co-driver should transfer as much of that route as he has been given onto his maps.

There will be cases where it will appear to have been a complete waste of time for the co-driver to have bothered first to have taken his maps along at all, and secondly to have laboured half the night before the off putting the route onto these maps. It only needs a last minute route alteration, possibly whilst an event is in progress, for any rally crew without maps to be at a very real disadvantage, even thrown into total confusion. On the other hand, I have competed on RAC Rallies, where it has not been necessary for even one of the numerous Ordnance Survey maps to have been opened by my co-driver, the road book being so comprehensive and foolproof. But a co-driver should always allow for human error in road book compilation—not an impossible phenomena.

Where a co-driver reckons that it will be possible for he or the driver to be able to take some sleep, however brief, the relevant parts of the route should be entered onto small cards, which can then be slotted into an illuminated ' automatic pilot ' holder, by which he who is driving the car can steer the correct route. The pre-prepared route-following instructions must be easy to understand and completely devoid of any ambiguity, and should also include the earliest and latest times the car can be booked in and out of the various controls that might crop up during the span of the instructions. It helps a driver to have such a route-following illuminated device as near into eye-line as possible, with a rheostat wired into the light power source for personal anti-glare tuning, and so cause the minimum of distraction.

TRIPMETERS

Twin tripmeters are a must for major rallies. The co-driver should check that the trips are accurate just before each event, in case the driver has had a different size of tyre or even an alternative final drive fitted. Where there may be some doubt about the accuracy of the instrument, such as when a co-driver meets up with his driver actually at the start, then he should make sure the spare gears are on hand if necessary for rapid substitution in the early stages of the event. These gears are tiny cog wheels, so he must take along the size of screwdriver needed to unlock the particular trip device's gears from their shafts.

Always at any rally start, there is an amazing and confusing amount of milling about, often involving crews in to-ing and fro-ing from one end of a town to the other. It is up to the co-driver to organise his driver during this signing-on process. If necessary, he must despatch the driver to assist at this time, but always keeping tabs on him to know where he is at all times. The driver can manoeuvre the car through scrutineering, whilst the co-driver masters the route and progressively complies with the various stamps of a start pass-card.

If the co-driver is at the wheel, he must hand the helm back to his driver a few miles before a special section, so that the driver can shake off sleep and run himself in. Most drivers take a couple of miles to limber up, particularly in the later stages of a long rally. If this is not done, then the time taken for a startled driver to cover the first few miles of a special section might be longer than it need be.

The all-thinking co-driver will also ensure that the side numbers on his rally car are periodically checked for legibility, and cleaned if necessary, so that the time keepers, particularly on the flying-finish lines of special stages, do not miss or mistake the number when the driver rushes his car past them at incredible speed! Sponsors also appreciate their decals being visible, so these should be cleaned at the same time. If ever a rally car is in a queue for a control or a special test, the co-driver should make the most of any breather to jump out and clean the screen and lights. This is usually within the regulations as it does not constitute a crew member working on his car effecting mechanical repair within the confines of a control area. A clean screen and lights do make a great difference to a driver's time over a special stage. The best possible visibility is also conducive to a driver being able to see what happens to the road, always a comfort to even the coolest co-driver.

Wherever the organisers are likely to be timing a rally car specially, as on a special section, the co-driver must take his own time too on a stopwatch. This is after all the only way he can tell how his driver is fairing compared to the opposition, the times of whom it is his duty to discover whenever the rally convoy pauses at a meal halt. It is also his only means of checking the accuracy of the penalty the organisers award when they post up the results of each stage at the main controls or finish.

CHECK-OUTS

Another task for the co-driver is to organise his driver into a check-out of the car's lights, horn and silencing prior to a final control where there is an official check of each car's compliance with a set of legal requirements. Often in the regulations there will be a list of penalties for various non-functions of the car's basic equipment. It is therefore in the co-driver's hands to check the points on this one, and, if possible, rectify blown bulbs and fuses if any. There is little point in giving away penalties for the sake of such a little thought, particularly if the penalties incurred for the non-operational bulbs are in excess of those that have just been won back from a rival over a whole series of special stages.

The longer the event, or the more international it is, then the more voluminous the paperwork. Despite increasing flexibility of inter-country travel, crossing frontiers in a rally car still seems to require all manner of carnet and insurance documents. Organisers usually pre-pay fees, if any, to save the rally crew any road time, and it is, thankfully, on the better organised events, simply a matter of driving straight through from one country to the next. Such paperwork is the co-driver's responsibility—most drivers will not want to understand at this stage.

Another tip with rally paperwork is for the co-driver to keep all the customs and car documents separate from the rally paraphernalia. As most drivers are prone to hurl their jackets off at the slightest sign of interesting territory looming up ahead, then the co-driver would be advised to safely store both passports. At least it is the one way to ensure that a driver does not stray too far, since passports are required to be deposited even in the humblest European hotel until the bill has been paid. The co-driver should make himself responsible for always collecting passports from hotel receptionists!

If there are any calculations of time, distance, fuel capacity, cost, or anything which is likely to tax the co-driver's harrassed brain, it helps for as much of the arithmetical slog to be attempted before the rally. For being bucked about a rally car's cockpit on the brink of collapse is not the most ideal background for a calculation, upon whose accuracy the fate of the crew may depend. Even the most lively brain will find simple addition quite an ordeal towards the end of a hard event.

On the larger events, all sorts of bits of paper will be thrust through the window from various firms anxious to let somebody know what they are up to. There will also be a good chance for the cockpit to become rapidly cluttered up with packets of giveaway chewing gum, boiled sweets, fuses, nuts and bolts, eye tonics, biscuits, and enough preparations to fill a larder shelf. The co-driver should quickly sift through all these goodies and bumph, and, despite any objections from a greedy driver, ditch all the surplus items as soon as the rally car is out of sight of the start control with its usual horde of representatives. After all, it does not do to openly discourage any commercial enterprise from taking any interest in the sport. Who knows, from their ranks, there might even be a future sponsor.

Co-drivers might find the various Guides to this and that country very useful to take along, the only snag being the obvious one of excess weight. Most Guides are usually impressively sized tomes, but still the information is likely to be relevant, particularly the detailed city and major town maps. The co-driver must decide between the virtues and the cumbersome disadvantages. If the event is abroad, then a phrase book is certainly worth taking along for the little space it is likely to occupy. Here again, it is up to the co-driver to think of this one.

Most co-drivers would agree that a detachable headrest is a welcome accessory on their side of the car, as is the comfort of a horn button, best mounted for foot operation. Particularly in hairpin country when rocketing down a narrow lane in daylight, the driver should not be expected to find the time for either hand or foot to sound the horn. This is another job for the co-driver, as well as always listening for the sound of an oncoming vehicle's horn. Co-drivers might even find bracing themselves between headrest and horn button a useful way of releasing any surplus anxiety.

4 The Service Crew

The service crew is a relatively recent addition to rally activity. There was a time when the only organised outside assistance for competitors on a rally was a communal baggage transport service, by which competitors had their prizegiving clothes carried on a direct route from the start to the finish hotel. On the rally itself competitors had to fend for themselves.

Servicing started off with the various factory teams organising their mechanics along a rally's route try to keep their cars going. Progress started to streamline this, until the mechanics themselves entered into their own rally, namely leap-frogging across country to work on their team's cars at various points.

Not very long ago, the purists declared that servicing on rallies was only ever going to be carried out by the professional teams. They were wrong. For commencing with the Home Internationals and spreading right down to some of the better club events, especially if there were going to be any special stages at all, the presence of service crews became commonplace. Indeed, any private owner who professes to take his rallying at all seriously must now have his own service crew. Some enthusiasts might consider that having a service crew is unfair but even if this increases the costs, as it will, if only one competitor was to have a service crew he would be running with a definite advantage. Perhaps it is the pace and intense competition of present-day rallying more than anything else that has been responsible for there to be a need for service crews. Without their presence, there would be very few finishers on any of the major rallies. It is not that today's rally cars are weaker, it is that with the expectancy of servicing along the route the drivers are harder on their cars.

Servicing involves all the skills, and more, of the rally driver/navigator already expounded. To many, servicing on rallies is an end in itself, the involvement being sufficient reward. To others, it is a way into the sport, being about the cheapest method of learning what is really involved before actually entering, at personal expense, as a real competitor. Service crew members have to be able to drive fairly fast, as well as safely. Driving along the right roads is just as important as it is competing in a rally, so the skills of navigation are necessary too. A service crew will have to drive on the limit, often quite a feat with an overladen saloon or estate car and as a result of this rigorous usage, many entrants seem to use hire cars for the task. This is very wise, if only few major rallies are contemplated, as at least with most hire cars maintenance will have more likely been carried out regularly. Also, hire cars are often changed frequently by their operators, so should be modern, and about the most reliable. Reliability is just as important on the service car as the rally car. It is also most comforting for any service crew to be ruthless at the wheel of somebody else's car following a rally rather than worrying about their own. The disadvantage of using a hire car is that it may not be exactly what is required. The service car must be capable of effortless high average speeds over diverse surfaces. A large saloon, or *Barge* as most rallyists affectionately called the BMC Competitions 3 litre service cars of yesteryear, is what is needed. An estate car is even better for load carrying. Ford have always used estates, or as their mechanics call them *Sheds*. Indeed, the layout of a Ford works service vehicle is the model of how to go about it for all those aspiring to do a good job servicing.

BASIC FUNCTIONS

At this point, it is as well to point out to the novice, that servicing is the least glamorous of the action jobs in the sport. Indeed, some of the ordeals in store for a service crew, particularly in really foul weather, are a rigorous test of even the most stolid devotee's dedication, the basic functions being as follows : to keep a rally car going, and occasionally to do this by repairing damage incurred by a driver's excess of enthusiasm to save the crew from tiring themselves unduly labouring on the car; and to use wisely every second when the rally car has stopped by the roadside service point. The most prevalent fault with those new to servicing is for them to crowd round their driver when he pulls up to ask him how he has fared, instead of working on the car. Whenever a rally car comes to a halt, there is always some small job that could be done. Servicing is supposed to be not just repair work, but also preventive maintenance, as well as straight-forward systematic checking.

The very first thing a service crew must do when their rally car pulls up at their position is to ask the co-driver firstly how long is available for work on the car, and secondly if there is anything in particular which needs specific attention. Knowing the length of time available is vital. If after a job has been commenced, the time arrives when the rally car should be in motion in order to be on time at the next time control and the car cannot proceed because the servicing has not been completed, is is the service crew who have failed. It goes almost without saying that any service crew must know their rally car. They must know exactly what is involved with the various jobs that might become necessary in the course of an event. They must also know how long each of these jobs is likely to take and as well as knowing how to do a job, is is important that they have the right tools available, and do not need to borrow them from the rally car. It is all too easy to let a rally car rush away without returning the tools. Any rally car once away from its service might just need the only tool that is missing from its set. The tools on board a rally car should be preserved for use by the crew to fix the car in the unfortunate event of something going wrong away from the service area.

In the same way that a service crew must know which tools are needed to carry out each job on the rally car, it must be clearly understood from the start who is responsible for doing the various jobs. Watching service crews in action is all too often an education in how a job should not be done. Many service crew members have a knack, if they are not standing bewildered by their rally car's arrival, of rushing to do the same job at the same time, with the traditional result of too many cooks spoiling the broth and the job maybe only being half-completed. This can be very dangerous if for instance the tightening of wheel nuts was overlooked in such a panic. The various tasks must be clearly delegated around the service crew. Everyone must know what he is supposed to do even if the stop is purely a routine one. If it is not, then a system must be evolved as to who does what first. Every service crew, however individualistic its members, must have a chief, who can direct operations—the foreman of the team. Often, with very little time to do many jobs, particularly when fatigue sets in, somebody must take charge military-style, however amateur the level of participation might be.

The co-driver should liaise with the service crew chief, or chiefs if the entrant is blessed with more than one service crew, as to where the rally car may expect service to be. The whole point is that if a rally car is expecting a service crew to be somewhere, it is there before they arrive, and not after they have gone through. A major failing with a newcomer to servicing is to be over-ambitious, resulting in failing to ever catch up with the rally. This is simply defeating the object of having a service crew in the first place, as the rally car will never really know whether they could expect service. Ideally, the co-driver should mark up his service crews' maps with the locations of the controls, the places where servicing should be done, and the route the service crew should take between these points. In addition, the co-driver should obtain a copy of the regulations for the service crew to read, mark, learn and inwardly digest, so that they understand especially the marking of penalties.

A time schedule is wise too, so that the service crew know what time, earliest and latest, to expect the passing of their rally car. But it is as well to advise any service crew to always stick to their position if the car does not show up right up to the point that the rally car would be out of time if it did arrive. Only if a reliable message of the exact location of their rally car in trouble is delivered by a passing competitor should a

22 Large estate cars make the best service vehicles. This one, servicing the Datsun team, has an extremely robust (and very necessary) roof rack to increase the total carrying capacity. Extra lights are usefully employed on such a rack to illuminate the working area.

23 One of the first considerations for any service crew is to take along everything that is likely to be required, but a great deal of system has to be employed. This model of service car layout, an estate car from Ford Competitions, utilises rows of drawers clearly marked up as to their contents.

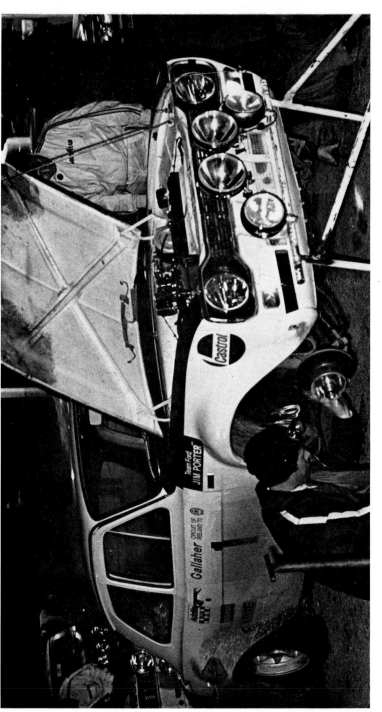

24 Private entrants can learn much by observing the servicing techniques of the works teams. Here, Ford use a quick-lift jack so that both front wheels of Roger Clark's Escort can be removed for a disc brake pad change. Note the works mechanic using a miner's helmet lamp, so that he can see what he is doing.

service crew take it upon themselves to start looking for the car, and so move from its position. The co-driver might be in the process of obtaining a lift from a passing car in order to come to collect some vital part that the rally car might need to become mobile. If he were to arrive to find no sign of the service crew he would not be pleased, especially if there was the slightest chance of such an action by him being able to keep the car in the rally. A service crew ought to hang on at its position until the rally car, or at least one of its crew members arrives, by farm cart or mule even. But if, a service crew receives a message to go back to assist its rally car, then it should do so by carefully retracing the route, so any chance of missing the stricken rally car is avoided, obviously being very wary of later numbers, still in the rally, and still in a hurry!

INVENTORY

Deciding what to take along on a rally, and, more important, what not to take, is not quite as crucial for service crews as it is for rally crews themselves. The weight problem is not so acute for a start. But what is taken must be well packed, so it does not destroy itself and the rest of the car around it in the hectic course of an event. Stowing service car kit is an art in itself. Knowing exactly where everything is packed when the job is finished is time consuming, but if a rush job is done in packing up the service car, it will undoubtedly show with chaotic capers by the crew on the event, and much burrowing amongst piles of mechanical jumble for something that will be needed in a hurry. Everything must be battened down to prevent it from flying all over the place. Partitions are a must for the separation of small items, whilst a service car cannot really have enough boxes, clearly labelled to identify their contents. Heavy equipment or parts logically should not be carried in the rally car if a service car is being taken along. Even in the service car, such items must be stowed as low as possible on the principle of the heaviest things fall the hardest. Welding bottles and trolley jacks can be very dangerous if they suddenly shoot forward at head level in an emergency stop. Such attention to detail also assists in the battle against making any service car

G

excessively top-heavy. Weight should ideally be distributed as evenly as possible and whilst roof racks are quite usual, they must preferably be the sturdy commercial variety, or at least really well reinforced touring ones, with added gusseting to prevent buckling. Roof racks on service cars will have to withstand a far more active life, often with much heavier loads, than on any holiday touring application, so they must be really well anchored to the roof. I remember all too vividly having the roof rack from my service car destroyed on one Circuit of Ireland when it came adrift on a particularly high speed humpback, scattering its load of tyres and lamps, and finally being squashed by a following service car, also in great haste to reach its next rendezvous. Perhaps if a service crew packs its own service car, it will at least know where everything is. Half the battle of order over chaos has then been won.

It might also be found helpful, where it is known that parts with short life expectancy will have to be changed during a rally, for the service crew to prepare sub-assemblies in advance if this is viable. I have known cases where to change one simple part, like a shock absorber, turns out to be a long time-consuming series of operations to dismantle and re-construct some carrier, where if a spare carrier had been taken along by the service crew, with a new damper ready mounted, it would have been a simple matter of really rapid substitution of a pre-prepared sub-assembly. The more jobs that a service crew can pre-prepare before the rally car actually arrives on the scene the better. When the rally car arrives, time might well be extremely critical.

With all this talk of working on the rally car, it must not be completely forgotten by any service crew that even the most basic service vehicle will require attention from time to time if it is to stay reliable. Indeed, with present day rallying becoming so specialised, and competitors even wanting to change tyres according to the surface conditions of subsequent sections, the presence of the service car with a change of tyres is becoming even more essential than ever. The preparation of the service car, if it is owned by one of the service crew members as is usually the case, should be as meticulous as a rally car. The service car is after all going on a rally too. It might need spares, so relevant ones should be packed. It has often happened, in the best organised circles, for a service car to be carrying virtually a complete rally car in parts, only to have to abandon the chase, letting its rally car down because of its own electrics or fan belt failing, no suitable spares being carried. If possible, it is very helpful if the same wheels and tyres used on the rally car fit the service car but if this is not the case, at least two spares should be carried. Tyres on the service car should be the all-weather variety for obtaining traction to depart rapidly from muddy service points. If the conditions warrant them, studded tyres ought to be considered as well.

In addition to keeping everything on board in some semblance of order, a service crew should also try to keep all their equipment as clean as possible. This is often a losing battle, but plenty of rags, water and hand cleanser are a must. Something to lie upon is very wise too, particularly as there seems always service to be done underneath the rally car. A service crew should attempt to clean spanners and equipment from mud and oil prior to packing them back on board again, if there is time. It might help to take along some spare dry overalls in case the weather conditions for working on the rally car are really bad. Then sets of waterproof over-overalls are sensible, rather awkward in which to work, though easily sponged clean and dry. As with the rally crew themselves, the proverbial rally jacket is standard equipment for service crew too.

SERVICE POINTS

The itinerary of a service crew should be such that they will have sufficient time to set up shop with only a few minutes to spare, and display clearly their own service sign, so that the rally car can spot this in plenty of time to slow up. That is if he has time to stop for service. It is as well, particularly in areas crowded out with all the other service vehicles, for signs to be duplicated, with one fifty yards back up the route, and another by the service car itself and, as a sign can be carried off by a souvenir hunting local, blown by a gale over a cliff, or simply overlooked in the rush to leave for the next service point, a spare one ought to be taken along. These service car signs should be on stout (but not too heavy or solid) board, hardboard being best as this seems to withstand storms, not pulping so quickly as cardboard. They should also be luminous, studded with reflectors or decorated reflective tape. Perhaps for the sign, by the vehicle itself, a lamp can be directed upon it, so the driver is given every opportunity to recognise that help is at hand. Some crews rig up bleeping lights, whilst others manage to build forward and rearward facing service identification boards around their roof racks.

Naturally, if at all possible, a service crew should try to select a service point near to the location the co-driver is expecting. This is more than likely to be just outside a control area, just before a special section, or just after one. Suitable places to work on a car will be at a premium and it is unlikely that there will be acres of hard-standing car park, just where it is most needed for rally servicing. Obviously, as hard and as level a surface should be selected as possible. It pays to be as near to the control or start point as possible, so the co-driver can wander off on foot to check the official time for himself whilst service work is being carried out. Slopes are very unwise places for servicing, especially if there is any jacking up to be carried out. If a slope is the only place, then chocks of wood or stones should be gathered to be on hand for the job of stopping the car from running away if work is done which necessitates lifting a corner or side of the car off the ground. The place chosen must be as safe as possible as far as passing vehicles are concerned. If the roadway is very narrow, one member of the service crew should be on hand to wave down rally traffic from running over a servicing mechanic, possibly partly lying in the road working on the rally car's underside.

The well organised service crew should be completely ready for the rally car's arrival, with jack and spanners all laid out in readiness. If a tyre change is a possibility, then the wheelbrace and wheels must be stacked ready.

If the service point is being set up at night, then plenty of illumination must be organised. Every service crew should have a spare battery or two, so plenty of hand-held lead lights can be easily rigged up. Old headlamp bodies, complete with light units, or fog lamps, make very good auxiliary lights for making service by night less of a problem. Battery powered hand lanterns are obviously most helpful too, whilst another good tip is for the service crew to park their service vehicle in such a way, that their headlamps illuminate the working area. If this is done, it might help to avoid a flat battery, if the engine is left running on a fast tickover.

Because strangers in the night have a distressingly human habit of being light fingered, whilst all the equipment is laid out in readiness for a rally car's arrival, one member of the service crew should sensibly stay outside the service car's cockpit to keep an eye on things. Also to keep the working area free of spectators, curious passing motorists, as well as to show other service crews that you have reserved your pitch, a cordon using lengths of wire or old clothes line is easy to arrange. Particularly when the rally car does eventually arrive, this helps to keep the public at bay : such professionalism also does a little to demoralise the opposition.

The rally car's jack and wheelbrace should never be used at a service stop, as these are all packed away in readiness for operation by the crew, as already discussed. The service crew is very likely going to have to lift up the rally car, at one time or another, to change wheels and tyres, or to work on the underside. For such occasions, small portable screw- or bottle-jacks are not really man-sized enough. A trolley jack is the best, even if this has to be borrowed from the rally driver's friendly local garage for the duration of the event. Ideally, two such jacks are best of all, for it is always possible that both ends of a rally car might have to be lifted off the ground at once, as would be the case in an all round suspension change. But two trolley jacks do take up a great deal of space, and of course, are extremely expensive items to purchase. As well as sturdy jacking equipment, axle stands are the best equipment for putting under the car once it is in the air, especially sensible as a precaution if somebody has to crawl around underneath to effect repairs. Jacks have been known to fail hydraulically or sink into soft ground.

On some events, it may be possible to come to some arrangement with a wayside garage for a rally car to use their premises and facilities for a service stop. Some of the factory teams often prefer to do this, or take over a yard or farm barn, where security for all their equipment is not so likely to prove a problem, and where they can work on their team cars without interference. This should all be organised by the co-driver as part of his forward planning, permission obtained, and the location of such places given to the service crew in advance.

Setting up a base service camp is particularly useful on events that involve rally cars passing through the same village several times, or where competitors return to the same finish town after each day or night's rallying, which has been the case on the Scottish for instance. Under such circumstances, major rebuilding jobs can be carried out with the best possible facilities on hand, whilst out along the route, where there may be less time available for working on a car for long, only routine checks and lightning patching up need be done.

MOBILE GARAGE

The service car should be a mobile garage cum mother-ship to a rally car. If it can be organised, then all the rally car's petrol requirements should be met by the service crew. This may be a great boon to a competitor if petrol supplies are few and far between enabling the competitor to travel along the route only needing to carry enough fuel to link up with the next service point, the saving on weight making for better stage times. It is also helpful for a competitor having stopped at his own service point, not to then have to stop all over again at the next petrol station just to fill up with fuel. Often at the main controls, there is an enormous queue for petrol not only of other rally cars, but spectators and the pack of service cars also. The competitor who has organised his own fuelling can run lighter and save himself what could be valuable, perhaps vital road time. The only snags with service carrying a rally car's petrol are safety, as well as the all too obvious one of the rally car becoming dependent on the fuel being available where he not only will expect it, but also really needs it. But even if the competitor does not plan to use his service car to supply his fuel, it should always carry plenty of spare fuel. It is possible, for the rally car's petrol tank or system to spring a leak, and for service to find the tank so low that, without a roadside refill, it is unlikely to make the next known open petrol source. It is also possible that the service car may find it difficult to find petrol stations open late at night on its route, which will be different from the rally one where no doubt the organisers will have made arrangements for certain garages to remain open. In such cases, it will be the service car who will need the spare petrol.

As a service crew might have no time to stop for refreshments if it is to keep to its schedule of service points, then sufficient food and drink ought to be carried to sustain its crew for the duration of the rally. Invariably, there will be long waits by the roadside anticipating the rally car's arrival time to come up, so it might be as well for a Primus to be carried so that hot food and drink can be consumed. On the really tough events, the rally crew will depend for its only refreshments on the service crew having prepared some coffee and snacks for them. On such events, the food and drink for a rally crew should be prepared in readiness, the service cockpit warmed up with the heater, so that the rally car's crew can shelter in comfort whilst the service work is carried out on their car.

Where there are official meal halts for competitors, *Parc Fermé* rules, with no work allowed on the cars, may apply. If they do not, then the service crew should make the most of this time, when the rally crew are refreshing themselves, by servicing the car. If the service crew arrive at the meal halt after the rally crew, then instead of joining them in the restaurant, they should discover what needs to be done to the car if anything and proceed with the various jobs outside.

It will be necessary for the service crew to snatch sleep when it can, but as soon as there is any possibility of the rally car arriving, then one member of the service crew must be sure to be ready awake. It may be that the rally crew will have insufficient time even to stop to say that they do not want or that they have not the time for service. One service crew member should be out of the car, as long as the weather is not too bad, so that the co-driver can shout all is well or unwell on the way past. If the weather is really diabolical, or the time span when the rally car might come through is very long, a scheme of horn blasting or light flashing must be decided upon, then the rally crew can at least let the service crew know it is them passing. This identification of a rally car, particularly if the car happens to be a Ford Escort or yet another Mini, is of obvious importance. Once the rally car flies past, the service crew should not be too despondent that it did not stop for any service, but should efficiently gather up their equipment, not forgetting the service boards, to make sensible haste to the next point where service is planned.

There are just a couple of points that are worth mentioning to anybody who might ever be a member of a service crew. The whole image of the sport with the general public is dependent just as much on the behaviour of the service crews as it is on the rally competitors themselves, the public not knowing the difference. The service car is all part of the rally convoy. So, bad driving, excessive noise, and, worst of all by service crews, leaving piles of old oil cans and litter will do much to harm the cause of rallying as a whole.

5 Car Preparation

The best crew combination possible will be completely wasted unless the equipment they are to use is up to scratch. In the same way as the people involved in rallying have to prepare themselves by developing their specialised skills, so machinery expected to carry a rally crew to victory must be in first rate condition.

ENGINE

Commencing with the engine and its preparation, it is no use anybody imagining that they will not be able to compete on rallies unless they have race tuned power units. Far more important than a commendable horsepower figure is the reliability performance, which should be unquestionable. So many novices to rallying, even if funds are really short, spend far too much on engine modification instead of straight-forward engine condition soundness. In fact, once an engine's condition is found to be good, then increasing its performance should come last in the chain of detailed mechanical preparation on any rally car; suspension, underbody protection, electrics, instrumentation, cockpit and boot content being more important.

However, assuming that a rallyist intends to thoroughly inspect and prepare his vehicle completely, then the really serious competitor must consider expensive preparation for his engine specifically for rallying. Once everything else is perfect, the crew knowing all the tricks of the game, then, and only then, as much power as the engine can produce, before the reliability factor is affected, will become important.

In the upper echelons of the sport, where rallies are won or lost by seconds on special sections, a driver will not want to handicap himself in the face of the evenly matched opposition by restricting his performance with a completely standard engine, even if its condition is known by him to be first class. For in such circumstances, the driver will only stand to beat modified opposition of similar experience and form in the event of their default, hardly likely to please himself or impress knowledgeable enthusiasts.

Starting off with the obvious basic need for an engine to be put into perfect running order, the only way to be sure that this is indeed so, is to remove it from the vehicle, dismantle it, and have a look. Those followers of the principle that what goes well enough should be left well alone might disagree. But mass production is mass production and rallying is an expensive business. Risks must only be calculated ones. So, however new a car may be, the engine should ideally be removed for a thorough inspection for wear or potential defect and for hand re-assembly. Re-ringing pistons, a new set of bearings, perfect gaskets and seals, as well as loving assembly might suffice, especially if the engine has already been modified as standard or by a previous owner but the benefits of all new tab-washers, big-end bolts, and nuts are only good sense whilst the engine is in pieces. Loctite on any thread from which a nut might rattle free, as well as lashings of Hermetite or gasket sealing compound all help to make an engine which is going to be going through it in a rally car application, stand a better chance of proving to be reliable and oil tight. Whilst an engine is in component form, the balancing of crankshaft, flywheel and conrods may as well be carried out. Again, whilst in pieces, however new, it pays to fit a new pump, uprated if possible, as well as a competition clutch assembly. Heavy-duty parts such as these are usually instantly interchangeable and although they are always far too much trouble to be bothered with when an engine is in place in a car and going well, once the engine is out of the car it should be a different matter.

As a matter of interest, such long established supporters of motor sport as Automotive Products, AE Auto Parts and Ferodo, all market components especially for the enthusiast to incorporate into his engine for the maximum amount of reliability. AP sell a whole range of Borg and Beck competition clutches and from Ferodo can be obtained an anti-fade clutch anti-friction disc, whilst AE Auto Parts can provide competition specification bearings and pistons for most popular cars likely to be rallied, under their brand names Powermax and Hepolite.

When making a standard engine more reliable, always remembering it is likely to be put under far more stress than the makers intended, particular attention must be paid to a simple component like a timing chain. Such items are taken for granted normally on a roadgoing application where the professional maxim from most garagemen might be, if it did not rattle fit it back to the engine again. Any such form of false economy must be avoided. Believe me, however extravagant this may appear, it will pay dividends—or rather the driver will not have to pay forfeit by his engine going wrong too frequently.

Before an engine is modified at all, attention must be paid to its cooling. The water pump and radiator ought to be most carefully checked and replaced if there is any doubt as to their condition, and although mechanically driven fans are known by the boffins to be power absorbing do not necessarily throw away the fan. However fast a rally car may be driven through the air, the radiator core can always clog up with mud, the through flow of air therefore being affected. Then there can always be much shuffling along in traffic queues, either through towns on the larger events or up to the start of a special stage, thus making boiling more likely if a fan has been removed. A mechanical fan is so much less likely to go wrong anyway than a thermostatically controlled electric one. Naturally fanbelts and pulleys must be in perfect condition, with regular renewing and adjusting of the fanbelt being a routine task for any rallyist. If possible, a spare fanbelt can well be fitted behind the pulleys in readiness to make a change more rapid. This is a particularly useful tip if the fan has been retained and threading a replacement belt between blades and radiator cowling is a time consuming job. As well as considering the water temperature, an oil cooler can be a very important addition to any rallyist's engine bay. With a sumpguard it is more likely than ever for the oil temperature to be way in excess of even a racing application, so an oil cooler is recommended for even a standard engine. Great care must however be exercised with its installation, so that the pipes and/or rubber hoses are not likely to chafe through. As with the water radiator, the oil cooler must be shielded from flying rocks and stones, ideally screened from missiles with a wire mesh guard.

If there is any likelihood of anything coming loose on a rally, the item should be drilled and wired to prevent this from occurring. Drilling and wiring a petrol pipe union nut and bolt may seem a complete waste of effort, but it only needs an under-bonnet petrol fire as a result of this happening, for the point to be all too vividly brought home to the novice—but in such an instance too late.

Chafing is a common cause of mechanical failure on a rally car. Special care should be exercised in the preparation of the engine bay to see that hose, pipe, and wire runs are unlikely to become rubbed through against each other, the engine or the bodywork. Often a liberal session with PVC insulation tape will suffice to sort out flapping wires and the like, whilst old hoses, cut up make excellent sheaths to slip over pipes or cables that have to move around. If there is any doubt at all with a hose or wire—replace it. Hoses should be changed regularly before they fail anyway.

It is not simply an old woman's preaching to say that oil, filter and sparking plugs should be changed frequently on any rally engine. These items are going to be overtaxed like everything else, so change them too as frequently as you can afford. In dusty conditions the oil will become contaminated very quickly, often needing changing in the middle of an event. Anyway, if the transmission is within the engine sump, the swarf build up may well be rather rapid. Changing the oil can often be rather difficult on many applications, access to the sump drainplug becoming covered over with a guard or undershield. Thankfully, many service stations now seem to have oil changing apparatus which operates via the dipstick aperture. Magnetic sump drainplugs are a good modification.

Also on the weekend (or after the rally) workshop practice, frequent sessions with a de-greasing substance like Gunk, are prudent. Only by doing this regularly will a loose or cracked component be discovered, and anyway, a sparkling engine always impresses local fans, who seem traditionally to infest any rallyist's driveway!

Even to carry out all the minor engine maintenance chores on a rally car, the correct spanners should be used. It is no good trying to skimp with just an adjustable any more. A comprehensive set of tools should be purchased. Knurled over nut corners, burred threads and hacked about screw heads do not belong in the world of serious rally engine preparation.

If a rally, anticipated on a programme, is likely to have any snow or ice about, then anti-freeze must be mixed into the cooling system and in addition, some spare top-up anti-freeze ought to be ready diluted with some water to the correct proportions, to be taken along so that a top-up is of similar consistency. Just to stop a radiator leak before it starts, a tin of a radiator sealer like Wynns or Radweld is yet another detailed tip that cannot do any harm, yet might just prove to be worthwhile, whilst radiator caps should be up-rated, by substituting the standard cap for one with a stronger poundage blow-off spring, to avoid a singing kettle at the first control. The cap lid should be carefully drilled so that it can be secured from possible loss by a small chain or wire, and it is sensible to do this to the oil filler cap on the rocker-box as well.

If the air cleaner is retained, the filter element must be frequently changed or washed out, particularly if a rally takes place in high summer. If the cleaner has been discarded, a gauze mesh ought to be fitted to the carburettor intake to prevent a stone entering the engine and causing considerable damage.

All these details of preparation might appear to be unnecessary, but, at one time and another, they have all proved to be of vital use to rally crews. Reliability, and being able to fix a fault in a hurry, is basically far more important than the power output of the engine. But, if all these tips have been followed, then it becomes important to become competitive by modifying the engine, though with moderation. Engine tuning for rallying must be dependent on the type of event that is being undertaken. The extent of the camshaft's lift must be determined by the sort of going the rallyist is likely to encounter. A full race camshaft will be useless for a set of special tests where thick mud or snow is known to be likely. Conversely, a mild set of modified engine components would be of little benefit for anybody setting off on a rally which incorporates really fast roads. Obviously, the competitor's individual budget must come into the exact choice of equipment. Engines once converted are far more expensive to run. As a general rule, they are less likely to be as reliable for as long as a standard unit. Extensive engine modification might also be ill-advised if the owner still requires his rally car to double up for ordinary road transport as well. But to win in the higher echelons of the sport, a modified engine will be required.

When a rally car's engine is modified, one of the more usual occurrences is the modification of the engine's power output, which invariably means the fitting of different carburation equipment. However, one of the very worst features, when cars have been modified in this way, is that invariably the throttle operation becomes tricky. The car should be taken out into rally territory so that the return spring used is not tuned to be too stiff. It must be one hundred per cent certain that the return action of the springs will occur. It has happened that some conversions in this department have been a disaster, because their linkages jump out at the first sign of a hump on the road. As a general rule, cables seem to work better than rods and linkages, nylon-lined outer cables making for the smoothest throttle response, undoubtedly an essential factor in icy conditions where indelicate throttle response could turn out to be disastrous. Float chambers must be checked in field trials too, to see that fuel surge is not a problem.

All sorts of usually reliable components tend to wear out more quickly when an engine is modified. Therefore, more regular checks will have to be made of the condition of hoses and engine mountings. Whilst drastic modifications to the induction apparatus will upset fuel consumption, which can in turn necessitate the carrying of more petrol, either in cans or by the fitting of an auxiliary tank, or even a larger one in place of the standard unit. Then larger or more carburettors tend to increase noise in a cockpit, so soundproofing may become essential for a crew to remain relatively sane on a longer event.

Converting any engine usually sets up a chain reaction for weaker links to need attention. There have been very few converted engines that have been truly trouble-free. It is only when a reasonable quantity of a certain engine modification has been produced and a production model ready-converted brought onto the market, that the rallying owner's problems are likely to be reduced to any forecastable extent.

A modified camshaft will push the power output of an engine up, but the pulling power of that engine at lower engine revolutions will have been sacrificed. The best type of cam-shafts for rally engines are those that increase the overall power, yet still at the same time benefit the torque output. If a race camshaft is fitted which does make the engine more intractable, then an alteration of the gearing may become necessary; either the ratios of the gears will need to be closer together, because of the narrow power band of any converted engine, or a different final drive ratio may be required.

For ordinary road use, an engine conversion is best if it always stays as a compromise, but to be ultra-competitive in rallying, the only thing that should matter is the car being as fast as is possible within the limitations of the terrain the rally has to cover bearing in mind the duration of that event.

All the detailed tips already covered naturally become even more essential if an engine has been modified. If an owner is sufficiently worried about his engine's power output being able to give him an advantage over a section of road of a few seconds, then attention to the finer details becomes even more important. Oil cooling for instance will be of more importance if the speed that the internal components of the engine are turning over is going to be increased by modification.

If modified components come from the special Customer Tuning Departments of the major vehicle manufacturers, like Advanced Vehicle Operations at Ford or British Leyland Special Tuning, then it is more likely that the consequences, long term, of combinations of items of their equipment will have been charted. Development work will have had to have been carried out to prove all the catalogued items, often under rallying conditions. For example, a need for engine mountings to be more rigid, but yet not too much so, will have been discovered, and so these will be available for customers to purchase. Although a tuning firm may claim astronomical power increases from engine components modified by their boffins, these claims are all too often only the result of figures given on their engine dynamometer and not assimilated from their experience in the field, ideally over several thousand miles. Real rally conditions can never be accurately simulated in a laboratory. Inlet manifolds, which might well be the perfect theoretical shape and length, might fracture through when a whole car and engine are bucketed up and down with typical rally special stage violence. Carburettors, which might be the best possible for power output figures on the brake, may be useless when subjected to shaking conditions, the modified engine turning out to behave worse than the standard unit. An exhaust manifold might well be the optimum shape for performance, but might be too low slung under the car to be practicable for rally conditions.

One of the main snags with modified engines in rally cars is that their movement will seem to be more exaggerated, so extra stabiliser bars are often wise. Also, the clearance between an engine's fan and a radiator core can turn out to be too little if the engine were modified. Carburettor trumpets on longer inlet manifolds can become all too near to engine-bay sides when the modified engine's power comes in and the unit moves excessively on its mountings.

It is often so much more sensible to merely change a rally car's engine for a larger more powerful one of the same make from another car in the range. If this is a known conversion, the engine will be less likely to be temperamental, reliability therefore more certain. For instance, a Cortina 1500 engine or a GT unit does work so much better in the Ford Anglia, even well after its heyday, than a modified 997 cc or 1200 cc engine. The torque, so useful in rallying, will be higher, and the power

25   Sometimes it may be more convenient for competitors to organise their own fuel dumps. At this service point, Ford Competitions rally engineer, Ginger Devlin puts in just the right amount of fuel necessary to take Roger Clark's Escort to the next service point.

26   If there is room, or if the service vehicle is powerful enough, the well-equipped service crew should try to obtain welding equipment. However, the advice of experts ought to be sought before using such equipment as it can be extremely dangerous.

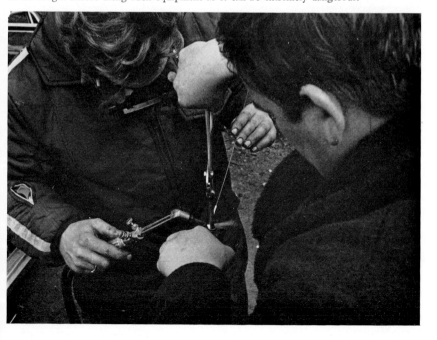

27 Tyre choice has become one of the most important variable factors of top class rallying. Latterly, various all-purpose rally tyres have been evolved for the private owner, as a direct result of development work carried out on factory rally cars. As a general rule, radial winter tread tyres are the best for most competitors who can only afford one set of wheels and tyres.

output often at least the same and sometimes even better. The same applies to an 850 cc Mini, where a standard 998 cc engine will be much more useful on any rally than a highly modified 850 cc engine, the reliability of which, at vastly increased engine revs, is more likely to be in question.

If an engine has been modified so that more frequent gear-changes are necessary to keep the engine screaming away, then it will be more tiring for the driver. Whereas a larger engine, instead of a highly modified ordinary one, will require fewer gearchanges, and so less effort from a driver.

A couple of points that may be worthwhile considering, are that when an engine is modified, its new car warranty will have been invalidated and that if the compression ratio is raised too high, the car will be unable to perform on anything other than the best petrol, which might be a problem in remote parts where octane ratings can be very low.

Whether an engine is standard or modified, or even if it has just been overhauled, an owner will not be giving it a chance if he does not run it in carefully. If all else fails and the re-build has been a last minute affair, always to be avoided in rally vehicle preparation, the drive to the rally start should be gently done as well as the first few miles of the event itself on the run-in to the meat of the event. The best rally engines are those that have been well bedded in, so that all the torque settings can be re-checked and the tappet clearances re-gapped. Before a rally, it is a very good idea for the engine to be taken on a run, so that the owner can be sure that it is oil and water tight, before finding out that this might not be the case on an event proper.

But with all this talk of engine modifications, the regulations for the events likely to be entered by the rallyist must be care-fully studied first. There may be different classes, as well as categories. This is likely to be the case on the larger events, where the current FIA regulations will certainly be enforced. Highly modified one-off engines may be perfectly acceptable for the top club rallies, where the awards are usually distributed purely on an overall basis, but on Internationals, unlimited modifications may make an owner's rally car ineligible. The

H

mysteries of the FIA's Groups One, Two, etcetera are complex and ever-changing. The best advice for those who do contemplate modifying their rally car, especially when the more important events are envisaged, is to study most carefully the relevant FIA Year Book, an annual publication. Here, all will be revealed as to whether seats, steering wheels and so forth can be removed; how many extra lights can be fitted; how extensive or limited the engine modifications may be; how many of the particular model will have had to be made—and so on. It is obviously important to read these regulations in the FIA Year Book fully before doing any preparation beyond standard to any rally car. For often, once trim has been torn out and a dashboard altered, it can be very awkward to restore these to standard; whilst actually having to replace metal from engine components is impossible!

Basically, the regulations are completely standard, modify the standard equipment, and finally substitute special components for standard ones. The usual rally paraphernalia can be usually added to all Groups. If there are capacity classes, reboring for larger pistons will be just as moot as it would in motor racing.

Here it may be of interest to lay out the rules that govern the classification, definition and specifications of cars taking part in international events. These are all in the FIA's Appendix J to the International Sporting Code, reams of detailed regulations, invariably subject, in part, to annual change. However, the general distribution of cars into different categories and groups remains basically the same. These are CATEGORY A: recognised production cars (numbers between brackets are those of the required minimum production in twelve consecutive months); *Group 1*—series production touring cars (5,000); *Group 2*—special touring cars (1,000); *Group 3*—series production grand touring cars (1,000); *Group 4*—special grand touring cars (500); *Group 5*—sportscars (25). CATEGORY B: experimental competition cars; *Group 6*—prototype sportscars. And CATEGORY C: racing cars; GROUP 7—two seater racing cars; *Group 8*—formula racing cars; *Group 9*—formula-libre racing cars.

The Groups that are most usually to be found on rallies are 1, 2, 3, 4 and 6, for whilst on British club events, anything goes as far as the extent of modifications, on internationals compliance with specified FIA Groups becomes compulsory. So the rallyist, who aspires to compete in events of higher status than the club rallies in which he may gain his grounding, is well advised to prepare his vehicle from the outset so it complies to the letter to one of these Groups. As for trends, there has been a move in recent years for private entrant's saloons on the more important events to comply to Group I, whilst most of the factory teams still prepare their team saloons to Group 2, grand tourers to Group 4, or build special prototypes to Group 6.

An official FIA Recognition Form is required to be carried by every competitor on international rallies, so that compliance with a particular Group can be checked for an individual type of car by the scrutineer. These forms are obtainable from the FIA via the RAC Motor Sport Division. All factory officially approved ' standard ' extras have to be registered on these forms and are checked on an event by the scrutineer. Whilst in addition, each Group has a long list of points and specifications that have to be adhered to by competitors in vehicles complying to these various Groups.

Wherever there are special stages the RAC insist, regarding the special stage as a speed event, that cars comply in the direction of carrying fire extinguishers of a specified size, boot and under-bonnet areas sealed off from the cockpit completely to prevent the possible passage of fire in an accident, and the fitting of roll-over cages of a laid down specification. The only advice to competitors in this direction of preparation is to read the RAC's Motor Sport Year Book, as well as the appropriate sections in the FIA Year Book—and to follow most carefully the various requirements.

TRANSMISSION

Modifying an engine will of course increase stresses for any transmission. The clutch for instance, will most certainly need modifying. If the power output is upped considerably, then the gearbox even might need uprating by the fitting of a competition unit, if this is available from the vehicle manufacturer. Once the strength of the gearbox is sure, then an owner might want to have just the right ratios for his engine's power curve. If weight is vital, then often such components as clutch and gearbox housings can be changed for magnesium ones.

Also, the axle and components therein might ideally need modifying so that they too might be more able to withstand the effects of increased engine power. On a front-engined, front-wheel drive car, thicker drive shafts may be available as well as stronger couplings. On front-engined rear-wheel drive cars, stronger half-shafts are important, whilst it may be possible to change the complete axle for a stronger one. The axle or final drive ratio must be the right one for the rally territory. There is no point having a ratio that will enable a rally car to be rocketed up hills to great effect, if the event is being held primarily on a plain where a really useful turn of speed down the straights will be more useful. The more revs an engine turns over and the longer it is subjected to this, the greater the wear and the greater the possibility of something breaking.

For club events, most of a competitor's time will be spent in the lower gears, so a low final drive is very wise. Top speed on such events is unimportant. All a competitor has to bear in mind is that the top speed on main road runs will have to be reduced, as it might even be possible to over-rev the engine in top gear.

SUSPENSION

All manner of sophisticated engine conversion equipment is of course completely wasted if the suspension on the rally car is not up to the tasks put before it. Of all the forms of motor sport, rallying is the hardest test of any suspension, the surfaces likely to be encountered being so varied for a start. There will be on occasions, stretches of rough, and because of the speeds at which a car may be driven on an event even the mildest patches of broken surface will tend to be a real challenge. Apart from the speeds that a rally car may reach, the very weight of a fully-laden machine at such speeds will test the suspension components.

Suspension should be firmer, and raised as well, if the events are likely to be rough. This may mean substitution of all the springs, or the introduction of packing pieces or blocks. In addition to the springs themselves, which will effect the ride height, the damping is of primary consideration. Changing the shock absorbers for heavier-duty competition ones is usually a straightforward fitting job anyway, so will not present any problems to the home mechanic. Where telescopic dampers are fitted, the units should be changed over, preferably for competition ones that are adjustable for wear or stiffness; and where lever-arm shock absorbers are the case, then different valves may well be used to help to keep the cost down, this having the convenient effect of up-rating the damping performance *in situ*. Cars fitted with Macpherson strut front suspension, combining damping and springing, can be improved greatly by the substitution of competition struts for the standard units. Competition struts will usually be wedged with a welded-in steel gusset to strengthen the join at the strut base with the stub offtake.

When obtaining competition springs for a rally car, the owner should ensure that he does not fit racing springs for although these will be much stiffer, and will help to cut out pitching and bottoming in the normal way they will, in most cases, reduce the ride height. If no springs, particularly made for rallying, are available, maybe there will be export ones in the manufacturer's catalogue, or even commercial vehicle ones from the same stable. There is no point in making a rally car's suspension too firm, for the jarring may shear through bolts, as well as shaking the rest of the car to pieces. Rally suspension should absorb rather than bounce—there should be travel.

For British Leyland models fitted with hydrolastic suspension, there are all sorts of ways in which an owner can modify his suspension for rough work. Initially, just a slight increase in pressure all round may be all that can be afforded. Then there are larger bump rubber kits for helping to reduce sink or excessive travel and in addition, auxiliary shock absorbers can be fitted at the front to augment the in-built damping characteristics of the standard hydrolastic displacers. If the budget allows, competition displacers are the best of all, with maybe the heavy-duty bump rubbers and extra dampers as well, especially useful on very rough events.

On certain models it may even be necessary to re-locate the mounting points of suspension components. For instance a damper mounting might on the standard car be too near the ground for it to be free from contact with rocks on the rough. Again, the standard layout of shock absorbers might not be the best for rallying, so can with advantage be changed. Such is the case with the standard Escort where the mounting of the rear telescopic shock absorbers at a slant can best be changed on rally Escorts to a vertical set-up, for the damping of the rear axle to be most effective. So, if the ultimate in suspension is required, then a turret conversion, even with all the welding in place of new box-sectioning in the boot, is worthwhile. The whole front suspension assembly on certain models can be re-fitted to a reinforced crossmember, often already fitted to export models.

PROTECTING THE UNDERSIDE

The standard location points on suspension might need modifying. If it is known, as will be the case on models of car that have been rallied a great deal, whether there is a weakness in a suspension's mountings, then the owner who takes his preparation seriously will prepare in advance so that a failure in this area does not occur. Although this is venturing into almost factory rally car preparation standards, if a bodyshell is known to be weak in a certain area, then it is best to weld in reinforcement before that car is permitted to leave the workshop for its first rally.

Welding up a rally car's bodyshell need not be so expensive, if the exact places requiring welding are known and with the reinforcement plates pre-prepared. As very few amateur rallyists will be able to afford welding equipment, this sort of exercise will involve a trip to a smithy. Knowing where to weld in plates is all a matter of discovering from campaigners of similar cars where the weakness points are known to be. Whilst welding is taking place all trim and carpeting near the affected area should be kept well clear in case the heat of the torch sets them on fire. In any case, an extinguisher ought to be kept at the ready.

On a rally car's shell, large washers ought to be introduced underneath all bolt heads, as well as where nuts abut against the shell. Shake-proof washers are worthwhile fitting, to prevent both bolt heads and nuts from slipping round. Where the shell's thickness has been increased due to plating, the threads of the bolts or attachments must be changed if necessary, so that there is sufficient thread extruding through the shell's holes for nuts to be easily made to bite onto the thread. Wherever possible, downwards pointing threads ought to be turned round, so that there are the minimum number of protrusions sticking out underneath the rally car to catch on rough roads. Lock nuts, and even Loctite, may appear to be all rather fiddling, but will pay off on a longer event where things are likely to rattle loose.

The suspension on any car is often the most ignored department. On a rally car this must not be the case. The suspension should be really carefully prepared and, after events, gone over most thoroughly. But welding up a shell to prevent suspension components pulling through will be considered to be breaking some of the FIA's rules for the various Groups. Reinforcements on certain cars are approved by homologation. The vehicle manufacturer will be able to tell an owner what he can and cannot do to his suspension, within the particular Grouping that interests him. Again for club events, nobody will worry at all. Of course it is cheaper in the long run for the bodyshell and the suspension to be prepared for rough road work, especially if a long series of events are planned during a car's ownership. Preventing a car's shell from buckling up is not only important on the event itself, it helps a great deal to prevent the car becoming a mobile write-off. The extent of preparation in this area depends on money, as well as the number of events envisaged, again a further question of money.

The preparation of the underside of a rally car is very important if the car is going to spend any of its competition life at speed on rough roads. There are rough roads and rough roads, but if any car in the rally has been prepared so that it can be driven with impunity over rough roads fast, then he, who is unable to follow suit through lack of preparation, is again at a very real disadvantage before he starts. Protecting the underneath need not be expensive. If an owner does not want to go to the trouble of stripping out all the vital pipework and wiring that might be underneath his car in the standard positions, he can quite easily bolt on some protective steel plates. Perhaps some thick rubber sheeting can be introduced between these plates and the car's underside to act as cushioning around the pipework. There are very few cars which have their vital pipes and wires running through the cockpit. So any car, which is to be entered really seriously on events, needs to be prepared by moving these services inside, so that they are safely removed from attacks by rocky outcrops. The usual services that trail about underneath a standard production car are front to back steel brake bundy tubing, the fuel line, the battery cable, and in some cases the main harness run to the rear-end illuminations too.

It helps to make the job an easier one if the underside can be made so that it is more accessible by using a garage's pit but if such facilities are not available, as will be the case no doubt in the average driveway, then ramps and axle-stands will do just as well, although having removed the vehicle's battery, the car can be tipped onto its side with the help of a few friends. Once in this position the pipes can either be protected with the plates as described above or they can be carefully detached from their chassis tabs. If there are rivets securing the clips to the underside these can be drilled out. If the condition of these service pipes and wires is in doubt once removed, or the removal is too difficult without damaging them, then a new set must be fitted instead. When they are run along the inside of the cockpit away from all the rocks and flying stones, care must be exercised so that they are kept well clear of hinging bucket seats and potential kicks from crew members' feet. The best place to attach a rally car's pipework is along the sides of the cockpit. It has happened that a particular violent rock can tear through the floor, or hit it with such force, that a brake or petrol pipe even with the floor between it and the road can become damaged. All pipes and cables should be carefully secured with clips, which should ideally be riveted in place rather than by using self-tapping screws, as rivets do not rattle loose in the same way as selftappers do during the course of a rally. On works cars, the clips themselves are often sheathed with tape to prevent them chafing and to grip the wires or pipes more securely. When pipes or wires are re-routed, they will have to run through panels, and so grommets must be used. It might help to glassfibre around these places to prevent each grommet from becoming displaced at a later date. Some preparers even run their pipes and wires through conduit, whilst others run them through lengths of hose pipe. The only snag with covering pipe runs completely is that if there is a fault on any of the lines, it will be difficult to spot the exact whereabouts of a leak or a fray.

The front to back hydrolastic link pipes on a Mini, particularly as it is so low slung, must be well protected and should ideally be routed through the inside of the car. The same goes for dry sump oil pipes, where the oil tank is in the boot and the oil has to be carried to and from the engine up front. Cars with radiators at the front and engines at the back must also have their water hosing carefully routed to avoid any potential damage.

Where it becomes impossible to re-route a pipe so that it is right up out of the way, then, in the case of bundy piping, sliding over the length of pipe, prior to the olive unions being sweated on, some plastic fuel tubing helps to offer protection that is not too bulky, yet is transparent. If it is too difficult a job to make a new run of pipe for this to be carried out, then sheathing pipe can be slit down one side, to be slipped round each pipe as protection and affixed to this with wire clips or tape. The brake hose runs, out to each brake, backplate or caliper, are dangerously vulnerable on any rally car. These should be disconnected first for protection preparation from rocks and the like, by feeding wire coil springs over their ends. The same goes for the clutch hydraulic hose running from the clutch pipe to the slave cylinder.

If there are any protrusions on the underside of a rally car that cannot be redesigned or eliminated by modifications, then an attempt must be made to protect them by tack welding or bolting on small tabs of steel plate to secure them from damage from underneath.

If any part on the suspension of a car looks as if it might buckle under rally strains, then it should be strengthened by gusseting each corner with a brace. The underside of a pressed steel lower suspension arm will be much stronger if it is built up with steel plate welded along its lower side. Vital brackets for the location of a link between a steel brake pipe and a hose should be protected with a bridging tab too.

Cars, where the battery or fuel pump is mounted low down underneath the car, should warrant especially careful protection preparation. Padding rubber should be fitted next to the unit, and the leading edge of the carrier, as well as the carrier, shielded with steel guarding. If the Grouping regulations permit it, both battery and fuel pump should be moved to safer locations. The lower sides of water and oil radiators, however high up these may be, can be vulnerable, so these too should be protected from possible attack by flying rocks from beneath, or for that matter from their cooling vents. Fairly fine mesh wire netting can be rigged up across the forward facing grille apertures.

One of the most vital areas in rally car preparation in recent years has been making exhausts strong enough to last out for the duration of an event. When an engine has been modified, making sure that the exhaust noise is not too excessive is of paramount importance, particularly on British club events, where the anti-noise regulations are the severest a rally driver is likely to encounter. Apart from the likelihood of antagonising any native who might not care too much to know that a rally is passing by his abode in the dead of night, the performance of an engine is likely to be seriously upset if the exhaust becomes damaged. For the well-being of the sport, and indeed to preserve any kind of future for it, rally cars should be as quiet as possible before the start of any event and, even more important, just as quiet at the end. The exhaust system will need to be prepared as thoroughly as the rest of the car for this to be so. There are various schools of thought as far as exhausts are concerned. Either they should be allowed to move about, or they should be as solid as possible, a piece of flexible pipe linking the relatively solid manifold with the rigidly mounted system. The decision on whether a system should be one welded into one piece or have the separatism of its components retained is another yet choice. For depending on the installation, it may be easier to pull a one-piece pipe and system off for ease of ' on-event ' repair. On the other hand, it might be thought preferable to still be able to attack items of the system separately for individual replacement. I favour the one-piece system with all the components welded together.

The leading and trailing edges of each silencer box should be skidded with small scraps of steel, so that they do not catch on any rocky protrusions, causing a silencer box to become ripped open. In addition to the units making up the system being welded together, it is also very important to double up on the system's mountings, so that however badly damaged the system may become at least it does not become lost in the night. On a really rough special stage, with both crew members wearing helmets, it is very difficult to detect a system dropping off.

Small snips of welding wire tacked onto the various system components linking them, and also acting as a second string attachment of the system to the body itself, work well to prevent a system from becoming totally detached from the mountings. The mounting rubbers themselves should be changed for heavy-duty variety, their number doubled if these are not available, or changed altogether for engine or gearbox mountings off another vehicle. Nylon nuts should be used to attach the system, as far as the clips to rubber mountings and the through bolts on the clamps, are concerned. The bolt heads should all be welded so that they are captive and the nuts should all be the same size, so that only one size of ring spanner is required for the crew to service the system on the event itself. All the nuts should be positioned, so that they are in no danger of being damaged by contact with rocks or earth.

If there is not a proprietary rally exhaust system available for a particular type of car, then any one-off must result in the silencer box, or boxes, being fitted as high up and as out of the way as possible. The rallyist might well have to make some sacrifices with such a system. Being so close to the underside of the shell it may cause a fair amount of resonance in the cockpit, as well as making the floor rather hot. Such sacrifices have to be made if it means that the rally car has a chance of remaining silenced for the duration of a rally. Noise meters, with penalty of instant exclusion, are not only used at the start of rallies, but during, and at the end too. It will be extremely annoying for anybody to have all but finished a really tough event without incurring too many penalties, only to be drummed out of the results with an exhaust that had been failed by a finish marshal's decibel meter. The limit, at the time of writing, imposed on competitors by the RAC's latest ruling on rally car exhaust noise, is no more than 87 decibels, and if anything this limit will be reduced in the future.

If one has to make up one's own rally exhaust system, then steer clear of all those supposed sporting silencers in accessory shops. Invariably their colourful paint finish and chrome tail pipes make for more noise along with all their claims of increased performance through reduced restriction of exhaust gases. Exhaust specialists will stock silencers of all shapes, sizes and weights, so boxes can be chosen that will be exactly the right size and robustness for the challenging job of staying intact on the underside of a rally car. Very effective silencing can be organised with a silencer across the back of a vehicle, right up out of the way. In addition, air cleaners will help to reduce the high decibel output of open induction trumpets, which in fact do so much to make a high powered rally car excessively noisy.

If there is anything else on the underside of the car that looks as if it could possibly come adrift, whilst working on the exhaust system before the sump shield is fitted, attention should be given to these points. Any amount of drilling and wiring of nuts and bolts cannot do any harm. The number one item however, of underbody protection equipment on any rally car must be the sumpshield. It does not matter what form, sophisticated or otherwise, this takes, but it must do its job—save the underside of the engine, or engine/transmission. Its presence will save an owner money and, in sheer peace of mind, can improve any rallyist's performance. All manner of devices have been used over the years to do this job, from old leaf-springs, which acted as a skid under a sump, to complete full-length undershields. Two things must be observed in the fabrication of such attachments. They must not, in themselves, act as too much of a protrusion, or else the vehicle's progress on the rough will be slowed up, and they must not be so heavy that the vehicle becomes weighed down to such a degree that it can hardly move. Somewhere along the line a compromise must be reached, where the sumpguard protects the sump, acts as a skid for the vehicle's lowest and most vital parts to slip over rough ground, is not too much of a weight penalty, does not restrict the suspension's movement in any way, and can be easily removed and refitted during an event if necessary.

Most sumpguards are made of steel. But some of the more expensive ones can be obtained, at enormous expense, made out of magnesium alloy, which is not only immensely strong but weighs only a fraction of the equivalent steel fabrication. As a matter of interest undershields made out of Dural are not a success. The material is certainly strong and light. It is cheaper than magnesium alloy, and unlike magnesium, not being cast, it can be worked more easily by a home mechanic. However the snag with this material is that it does tend to become worn away far more quickly than steel or magnesium alloy.

Whichever sort of sumpshield is fitted to a rally car, it is very wise to insert some hard rubber between the top side of the guard and bottom side of the casting being protected. This will help to cushion the effects of a particularly violent crunch underneath, which might, if it were violent enough, push a whole area of the guard up with such force, that it could be damaging to the casing without the presence of rubber padding. Also, as long as the possibility of a fire is slight, it is most helpful to ward off small pebbles becoming lodged between the guard and the sump, if quantities of sponge rubber are packed in around the edges of the guard to fill the gaps. A stone lying on the top of a guard can be just like a drift being forced through a casing if the guard were knocked upwards with any violence. To prevent the rubber pad from gradually vibrating out of place, it should be taped in place, before the top side of the guard becomes smothered with mud and oil. On some installations, an aluminium tray will help a great deal to contain and locate such a pad.

BRAKES

Although in theory the quickest way for a rally driver to cover a piece of road is not to brake at all, in practice the brakes and braking system, even of a standard car, deserve special attention. There are very few standard braking systems on the market that seem to be able to cope, and keep coping, with rally stops. It is not the systems themselves that are usually at fault, but the lining materials used on standard production cars. Brake linings have to be a compromise that will enable the ordinary owner to find the effort required to be well within his, or her capabilities. Standard brake linings do fade when they become hot. It has been a fact of motoring life for years, and it will stay that way. The rallyist, along with his other special preparation, should look very closely at his brakes. First of all, they must be in first class order. This does not mean that a cursory glance to make sure that there is no fluid leakage and that adequate anti-friction material is present on pads and linings will be sufficient. The bundy steel brake pipes as well as the hoses must not be overlooked. They too become fatigued and should be changed occasionally. New seals must be periodically fitted to all wheel cylinders and the master cylinder should be overhauled regularly, either with a repair kit or by replacing the whole unit. The advantage of changing brake components for new ones is that it does mean that the cylinder bores and pistons are renewed in addition to new seals throughout.

Brake calipers on disc brake installations really do have a rough time. Often these vital components are stuck out underneath in line of fire from flying rocks thrown up by the wheels. They should be checked regularly for tightness, as their attachment bolts stand a very good chance of being knocked loose. Earth and mud should be brushed off too, so that a check can be made after a rough event for any cracks on their surfaces. Although new piston seals can be obtained for calipers, it is far more sensible to exchange them for factory overhauled units instead.

Both Lockheed and Girling operate Competition Departments for their competition customers. So hand-checked units, whether these be production examples or special competition one-offs, can be purchased by the bona fide rally entrant, but such special equipment and service is really only likely to be of real benefit when major events are being tackled regularly. Again competition brake linings and pads are available from such leading specialists as Ferodo for virtually every type of car likely to be rallied. Most competition anti-friction materials might have to be warmed up before they can stop a car at all, so any special instructions for bedding-in must be carefully followed. Their presence is sure to completely alter the feel of a brake pedal, some competition linings being extremely hard, yet others only requiring the slightest foot pressure when they heat up.

Naturally with really hard pads or linings, the disc surfaces and drums must be checked frequently for excessive wear. Scored discs should be dismantled, refaced or replaced, whilst drums found to have grooves in them, should be turned smooth again on a lathe. To be really fussy, replacement in these areas is the only real way to be ultra-sure of the surfaces, on which the anti-friction materials have to bear, being as consistent as possible.

If many events are being planned in mountainous areas, especially if the vehicle being prepared is notorious for overheating its brakes, then special efforts should be made to cool the brakes in some way. Tips to do this can be copied from the world of motor racing, with vent holes in the rear of backplates, holes in the drum faces, finned drums, or ducts to scoop cooling air onto each brake. If there is any chance of any stones flying inside a brake drum when such holes have been cut, then gauze must be used to prevent this from happening.

It would only need one small pebble to slip out into a brake for the most disastrous braking performance to occur. In between events brake drums should be removed and cleaned out. There will most likely be large quantities of brake lining dust which, by its increasing presence, can upset braking. A garage air line is the best means of blowing out the dust from calipers and drums, prior to a detailed examination being made.

Many people imagine that brake fluid need never be looked at, apart from maintaining its level. This is a fallacy. In rallying, the hydraulic fluid will remain hotter far longer than it is ever likely to become under racing conditions. To maintain its viscosity and so its efficiency, it must ideally be changed regularly. Besides, small particles of brake seal will contaminate the fluid in time so, like engine oil, it too should be changed periodically. Once fluid has been pushed up to boiling point, then it should be changed. If ever part of a brake hydraulic circuit becomes damaged and air enters a system, then the old fluid should be bled through to rid the system of any minute air bubbles. If a pedal is very spongy, this will mean that there is air somewhere along a brake line; aerated fluid will mean a most insensitive feel to any set of brakes.

Also, once pads or linings have been really cooked or set on fire, they should be changed at the first opportunity. On a really hectic event, this will not usually be possible. But as soon as a rally car is back in the garage afterwards, linings and pads should be changed, along with seals and fluid. Sometimes oil can leak from an axle seal or grease exude from a wheel bearing onto the lining materials. They should be changed. Also, glazed or crazed surfaces on linings or pads indicate that their maximum efficiency has been impaired by excessive overheating.

The pros and cons of brake servos are always guaranteed to be a controversial subject amongst rally drivers. The force required by a driver's foot to retard his car is dependent on the individual's strength, aptitude or lack of nerve to have the need to brake in the first place. Certainly, a servo helps to reduce the fatigue aspect of repeated braking, so often neces-

28   The under-bonnet area of any rally car must never be ignored. Again straightforward
efficiency and servicing comes before appearance consideration. It is a good plan to install
some sort of illumination so that work can be carried out on the engine without needing a
torch. On this Cortina Lotus example a bracing bar across the engine bay to reinforce
the strut location.

29   The fitting of relays into switched auxiliary circuits should be considered a priority
in electrical preparation on any rally car. These should be fitted in such a place, that they
can easily be bypassed for emergency purposes, or replaced altogether, if time permits.

30 Having the best auxiliary lights, as well as high performance headlamps, is entirely wasted, without their being properly set up on a beam setter. Here, Cibie Rally Lighting expert, Gerry Wheatley adjusts a customer's Biodes.

sary on a long tortuous descent. Perhaps any such gadget that helps to cut down fatigue and make a driver less tired should be encouraged. However, there are three points against a servo. It is something else to go wrong; it is extra weight; and it usually reduces the sensitivity of brake feel. Anyway with the latest anti-fade brake lining materials, such as Ferodo's DS11 pad material and VG95 lining compound, once these are warmed up the effort required by a driver on the pedal is negligible.

It may be possible to uprate the brakes by changing part, or all, of the system for a later specification, or for a set of brakes as fitted to a more powerful car from the same manufacturer. Carrying out a conversion of this type must be properly researched before it is undertaken. The brake and vehicle manufacturers' technical service departments ought to be consulted, in case there is some sound engineering reason for not carrying out the conversion. If it is possible, they will have charted how the conversion brake equipment ought to be set up, as far as which pressure limiting valve for front to back balance works the most satisfactorily. A driver may want to experiment by altering the limiting valve, so that the rear brakes can be made to lock up earlier or later, as he may find this more comfortable according to his particular driving technique. The balance of a set-up of brakes will depend too on what sort of drive layout and weight distribution is in evidence. If, once weighed down at the front end with lights, a lamp bar and an enormous undershield, a car tends to suffer from the front end locking up under braking, there would be a case for the driver to want to change the brake balance, so that the backs lock up a shade sooner. And again, if a car has its light rear-end wheels lock up at the first touch of the brake pedal, then the balance ought to be altered too. Sometimes the standard brakes of a car, although perfectly all right even under the occasional extreme condition, are thrown completely out by the abnormal loadings of a fully laden rally car.

Most performance cars in recent years have been fitted with dual hydraulic brake circuits for fail-safe reasons. If a model of car is being prepared for rallying and a dual circuit is not

I

part of the particular standard equipment, then the owner would be wise to consider making the conversion to two circuits a priority task. On the rougher rallies, a torn brake pipe or a damaged suspension corner is always a possibility. If a loss of brake hydraulics were to occur on a downhill section, then a car might stand some sort of a chance from disappearing over the edge as a tight corner requiring definite retardation by the brakes loomed in sight, if two brakes out of four were still able to function independently. Converting many production cars to dual-circuited brakes can be carried out by the substitution of the mono master cylinder for a dual outlet one. If there is not a suitable unit available from the relevant brake component manufacturer, then it may have to be a case of some ingenuity being necessary to fit a second master cylinder alongside the existing one.

With the advent of disc brakes on all hubs, the importance of the handbrake for rally drivers has diminished, it being very difficult to make a handbrake really bite onto a disc. In days of yore, the handbrake was almost as important as the gearlever. The handbrake turn is all part and parcel of the rally driver's legend, its big advantage, apart from its basic function of being able to hold a vehicle well enough for parking to be safe, is that it can be made to swing one end of a vehicle in relation to the other. The skilful driver will know, to a tenth of an inch, exactly how to exploit the handbrake on his vehicle. The handbrake to the master rally driver should be like a lasso is to a rodeo star. On a front-engined rear-wheel drive car, making the handbrake have any positive effect necessitates a smart depression of the clutch foot just prior to the application of the lever. On a front-engined front-wheel drive layout, the rear end is usually trailing, so the handbrake can be easily made to lock the rear wheel at will, and by holding on, or reducing the grip of the brake, the whole of the rear end can be moved across the road, or stopped from doing this. On rear-engined rear-wheel drive cars, an application of throttle causes and varies the extent of the tail moving out of line more effectively than using the handbrake. The real opportunity for it to be used effectively by a rally driver in anger is to negotiate a hairpin, or to change direction rapidly, where there is neither the time or the room for a shuffle. With discs, as well as hard competition linings, even perfectly adjusted, the operation of a handbrake will require a titanic effort. The maximum amount of leverage possible has to be organised, which can even mean lengthening the lever itself and maybe strengthening it too. The lever can be fitted with a grip for convenience. If it is not 'fly off' in its operation it ought to be converted so that the ratchet does not lock on willy-nilly when it is applied on the move. This can be done by eliminating the ratchet altogether, or merely by drilling a hole through the lever grip end, so that a pin can be inserted to restrain the ratchet release button in the depressed, and so released, position.

Handbrake cables must be serviced along with the other grease points. Their runs must be lubricated, kept free of mud, and continually checked for free movement. On the rougher events, the handbrake cable and its runners are likely to suffer on a low-slung conveyance, so more frequent attention may be necessary. One other important point to observe on any handbrake installation is that in the event of a hydraulic failure, the handbrake with its mechanical linkage, may be the only thing to prevent a car and its crew plummeting brakeless into a wall, even if it just slows the car up sufficiently to scrape round the bend.

Cars whose systems are not fitted with competition specification brake fluid should have the fluid changed. Disc brake fluid has a higher boiling point than conventional brake fluids, so should be used, even on cars fitted with all drum systems. Major suppliers of brake fluid, like Girling, Lockheed and Duckhams all market suitable brake fluid for competition applications as well, whether the systems are all drum, all disc, or a combination of the two.

WHEELS AND TYRES

Most standard wheels are perfectly suitable for rally use. The main consideration for any wheels, as far as their suitability for rallying goes, is that they must be strong enough. The safety aspects of wheels cannot be emphasised enough and appearance should definitely be secondary. After robustness must come the other factors such as weight and size of rim. There are a glut of fancy wheels on the enthusiast accessory market at the moment. Most of these are entirely suitable for ordinary road use, but rallying can be rough, wheel centres having to withstand excesses of pull, and wheel rims often having to retain their shape even after mile after mile of rock bombardment. Wheels that merely look the part should be avoided. Invariably lumps will be knocked out of their rims all too easily if of the cast variety, or their rims will bend double at the first sight of a log if aluminium. Only on rallies where the going is guaranteed to be smooth will such wheels suffice.

Amazingly the novice often imagines that he simply must obtain wide wheels before he can even start to put up competitive times on events. There is little point in over-rimming any car, unless the power is amply available to drive the increased rubber area. There are other factors to be taken into consideration too. More rubber on the road will mean more strain for the suspension, the steering mechanism, and, in particular, the arms, wheel bearings and studs. Wider tyres will not necessarily fit under the wheel arches without there being insufficient clearance. Wider type walls can touch suspension components. This may not look as if it will happen when a set of wide wheels and tyres are offered upon the studs with the car stationary, but once that car is in motion, particularly under rally conditions, tyre rubber could lock up on the bodywork or suspension.

As with any mechanical modifications, the vehicle regulations from the FIA for the Group under which the owner is interested in competing must be consulted to see whether wider wheels are permitted. Most of the popular rally cars will have alternative wheel widths homologated as approved substitution accessories for the private owner. With luck, factory cars will have already carried out any development necessary through fitting wide wheels, and discovered the snags if any.

If wheels are to be really wide, it may be necessary to fit

wheel spats to cover the exposed tread area of wider tyres—a necessary legal requirement in most countries. These can either be added to the sides of the body above the wheel arches as eyebrows, or they may require fairly extensive modifications to the bodywork on all four wings for the welding in of complete wider wing spats. Spats in glassfibre or metal may be proprietary items on popular cars, where a complete kit of all the parts required may be obtainable. If this is not the case, and the job is beyond the owner carrying it out himself, the modifications may prove to be expensive in the hands of a coachbuilder or panel beater. But many rallies have been won, they will continue to be won, by cars without bulbous wings and racing wide wheels. These items are really only vital to the man who must have everything, as well as in the higher echelons of the sport, where the rat race of being competitive make such modifications standard equipment. Besides in snow and thick mud, thin wheels and tyres achieve better bite for traction and vital steering.

Where spats are added they must be securely attached to the body as there will be occasions even in the best driver's hands when the car may brush along a bank or slide amongst bushes. The spats must not be able to come adrift too easily under such circumstances. Self-tapping screws are the most convenient way of affixing such spats in place, but these do tend to shake loose on a long event. Ideally, spats should be glassfibred in place onto the body sides. Rows of holes drilled into the body for screws very quickly attract rust; the only real advantage of screw attachment for spats is that, being relatively temporary, it will be much easier to restore the car to standard prior to sale, the holes being fairly easily filled in again.

The low weight of some of the Minilite magnesium alloy wheels that so many serious competitors seem to use all over the world, is not to be ignored. Such wheels, apart from being several pounds lighter than their steel equivalents, are very much stronger. It is possible to drive a rally car thus equipped for several miles on a flat tyre, even when the damaged tyre has detached itself from the rim, without the rim splaying out as it would undoubtedly on a steel version. And apart from reducing the unsprung weight at the hubs, magnesium wheels are a great advantage, in that on a rally car where usually two spare wheels are carried, the weight reduction is very worthwhile.

The greater brake cooling of a spoked alloy wheel is also worth having. Indeed, there have been rally cars that have suffered very badly from brake fade, which has been cured simply by changing solid disc styled steels for a set of spoked alloy ones.

The serious rallyist is well advised to avoid all temptation of saving money on wheels by opting for widened steel ones, which have been modified by the inclusion of steel bands welded into their rims. Although their manufacturers may claim that their welds are stronger than the metal on either side, their fitment by those going rallying, is not to be recommended. In any case, scrutineers at rally starts are becoming more and more against passing cars fitted with welded up wide wheels.

The knock-on, knock-off wheels came to rallying from the real old days of Sporting Trials and road racing, where their appearance, as well as facility for speedy roadside wheel changes, were considered vital. On certain events, where several changes of tyre may be necessary, a knock-on device on each hub and appropriate wheel centres, to cope with being locked in place by a spinner, may be a wise modification. But this degree of sophistication is hardly the province of even the wealthiest amateur. The only thing, quite obviously, that can happen with knock-on spinners is that they have been known to come undone under rally conditions. So, if they are fitted to a car, the tightness of the spinners must be regularly checked by the crew, whose safety may be in jeopardy. Such famous rally cars as the Austin Healey 3000 used to use wire wheels, but surprisingly these wheels are not as flimsy as they look. They hardly shroud the brakes at all, but they do need frequent maintenance, with the spokes constantly requiring tightening up and replacing. Some drivers actually prefer the feel that wire wheels give them, in that they find the slight flexing of the spokes agreeable rather than disconcerting.

The tyre is one of the basic ingredients of rallying. The

actual choice of which tyre to use for which event is variable even on the humblest club event. The decision as to which tyre suits a particular car, and which tyre does not, is more akin to which brand of cigarette is best. There will be certain basic types of tyre which can be said to be what is needed for certain types of event or, on the longer events, for certain parts of the route. But the exact brand or tread design to be used is, in the final analysis, a personal choice. Indeed, under the extreme conditions of the ice, snow, thick snow, patchy snow, slush, grit and tarmac of a Monte, the variations of tyre—tread as well as stud, are always a nightmare even to the most knowledgeable tyre technician, where selecting exactly the right tyre for each particular test is as precise a business as it is for Arnold Palmer to decide which iron he should use for the next green.

So important has rallying been to the tyre business that whole trends of public tyre buying have actually been determined by the tyres that rally drivers use. The radial tyre was first used in any quantity by rally drivers, who found that they could drive faster, in safety, over unfamiliar roads on such tyres, and so it was that initially ' press-on ' types on the road were catered for by such ' rally ' tyres. Later the emphasis was switched by the various advertising campaigns to ' Rally drivers depend on . . . and ' Tested under rally conditions ' to ' get home in all weather conditions as safely as possible ' with such and such tyre.

Some form of sports tyre must be fitted for rallying. The tyre ought to be reasonably thick to withstand possible rupturing through stones and the height of the wall should be fairly low too, for the tyre to be as stable as possible. Lately there have been several extremely good low-profile crossplies introduced, which tend to be fairly wide, very strong in the wall, and offer the car many of the characteristics of a racing tyre. Perhaps the best tip for any beginner is for him to take a look round the leading cars at a rally start to see which tyre the experts are currently using, before following suit and purchasing the same tyre.

Naturally, any spare wheels should be fitted up with the

same type of tyre as fitted to the running wheels. The same sort of care should be taken with correct tyre pressures, as would be the case if the car was racing. If pressures differ from front to back, then the spares being carried on board the rally car, as well as any being taken along by a service crew, ought to be marked with the pressure most clearly.

As a broad generalisation, road treaded tyres should be obtained for road rallying and winter grips for events where loose surfaces are going to have to be traversed competitively. Obviously, there will be overlap. For instance a town and country tread pattern is to be advised, even for a road rally, in really bad weather conditions where some of the roads used are likely to be covered with mud or snow. Also in high summer, a road tread pattern would be completely suitable for off-the-road rallying on special stages, where the going, although loose, is at least likely to be relatively firm under wheel.

There have been attempts, because of the fantastic demand by rallyists for an all-purpose tyre to be marketed by some of the major tyre companies. Goodyear, for instance, produce their Rally Specials in popular sizes, which give good service on all the various surfaces a rally driver may encounter, yet are suitable for use by a driver for ordinary road use as well. The purchase of such all-purpose tyres are most helpful for impoverished devotee to keep within his budget as only the one set of wheels are required—a very real saving, particularly if expensive magnesium wheels were being used.

As more and more events are determined on special test performances, so the tyres used are tending to become more specialised. If the stages take place in the forests, then winter tread radials will be the wear, if around race tracks, up hills, or on closed tarmac public roads, racing tyres. The factory teams, if the event is vital to them, will even vary what sort of racing tyre they will fit, according to the texture of the tarmac surface, as well as the weather. As a rule though, where racing tyres are used by a works team, they will tend to opt for wet weather variety so that if there is an unexpected shower or a stream crossed the road, the presence of some tread across their wide tyres will at least offer some resistance to their cars floating off into the scenery. This progress regrettably puts up the costs for the private owner if he wishes to remain competitive.

On winter events there is the added complication on the tyre front of studs, which thanks to their Scandinavian competition origins, are available in all shapes and sizes. It is through rallying that well equipped motorists in European countries, in which snow is a fairly common winter hazard, now equip themselves in some quantity with studded tyres. There was a time when the studded tyre would not last five minutes if a stretch of tarmac came up in the middle of a supposedly snow-covered part of a route. These days are over, the latest studs having been developed so that they can withstand all the year round usage if required.

These studs can be simply fitted by a tyre dealer with a stud gun. So great has been the European demand that many winter treaded tyres are now made with stud holes already premoulded in their tread blocks. The studs can be fitted so that they cover the tread area fairly extensively, or simply encircle the tyre in two or more bands. Lightly studded tyres make very little noise when a car, thus fitted, is driven on tarmac, the studs staying in place even over quite long road mileages. The more studs that are fitted to a set of tyres, the greater will be the advantage in bad weather. Studs will make quite a difference to the sort of speeds at which a car can be driven on ice covered roads, especially as far as braking is concerned, the stopping distances not being all that much worse than they would be on a completely dry road surface.

There are different lengths of stud available, according to the depth of snow or ice that has to be conquered. However for really thick ice, the experts will be seen using chisels, which are so specialised and spiked that they would very quickly become blunted or torn out from the tread if they were used in conditions other than those for which they were specifically intended.

A British competitor will be unlikely to encounter the many sophisticated winter tyre alternatives, which will never really be used in any quantity in club rallying, or even on any of the major rallies held in the British Isles.

The most upsetting side to tyres in rally preparation is that they have to be discarded before they become worn out. It may seem a waste of money for an enthusiast to change his tyres between events, when there is apparently still some tread left but time may not be available to change the tyres halfway through an event, when the rest of the tread has been finally rubbed off. Special care should be taken between events for a thorough inspection of the condition of the tyres. Treads should be examined for bad cutting, whilst the walls, especially the inside ones, should be checked for cuts or bulges. Any tyre whose structure is in any way in doubt must be changed. For the cost of a new cover it is hardly worth the risk of a blow out, apart from the time lost on the rally itself when the crew has to make an unscheduled wheel change.

Any rally car travelling in winter used to carry chains on board to prevent it from becoming stuck in snow. Nowadays, chains are almost a thing of the past, only ever being used on winter rallies which cover roads on which studs are forbidden. But winter tread tyres and the wider use of limited slip differentials have meant even in the thickest snow that chains are really an anachronism. In any case, the time taken to fit them may mean more in penalties than would be the case if a rally car was slightly delayed by a reduction in traction.

Far more useful for any rally driver to take along with him on events are anti-slip boards for use in de-ditching. These can be put under the drive wheels to give the drive wheels sufficient traction to extricate the car, a few feet at a time. The best boards for this job are serrated ones, which can bite into the slippery ground on one of their sides, spread over an area so that they do not sink in, and also offer a serrated finish for the drive wheels upon which to grip. The amount of room a pair of boards like this will take up is negligible, being much easier to stow than chains for a start but, even so, such accessories have no real place in a rally car's boot on anything other than a real winter classic.

ELECTRICS

One of the areas of rally car preparation most taken for granted is the wiring. The thinking is often that if the electrics all work once they will continue to do so. But all the electrical components do need regular checks to make sure that all will remain well on the event, where a failure can be just as ruinous in time lost as if something went awry mechanically. A further problem is that the electrics on a rally car are only thought of as the additional wiring and accessories specifically for rallying.

The standard equipment should be regularly taken off the car and either exchanged at an auto-electrical specialist for factory exchange units or overhauled in the specialist's workshop. Preparation to such detail may again seem far too much trouble to the novice, but at least such preventative maintenance of distributor, starter and wiper motors, dynamo or alternator, control box, as well as regular checks of the battery will do as much as possible towards making any car electrically reliable. Regular rebuilds of these units will ensure that all bushes and brushes are replaced before they reach a worn out state, which can all too easily precede failure. Excesses of high engine revs for long periods of time will tax any standard rotational electrical units, so this sort of attention becomes even more necessary, whilst vibration can play havoc with the plates and links inside a battery.

Before any of the basic additional rally lighting is hung onto the car, it is a good idea to calculate the total electrical load a set of auxiliary equipment will pose for the standard power source. Any rally car with its basic lighting equipment alight, as well as a heater motor and map reading light, having to run off reserves of current stored up in its battery because the dynamo is unable to cope, will be unlikely to last the night out. A rally car's battery must always be capable of turning an engine over sufficiently briskly for a restart to be possible.

The most important electrical conversion the rallyist may have to make is to change the dynamo or alternator, fitted to his vehicle as standard, for one with a higher output. If the car has a dynamo he may wish to replace this and its control box for an alternator capable of producing more current to cope with the additional electrical load of his rally equipment. The other advantages of an alternator are that it is better able to withstand high engine revs, as well as being able to keep the right side of the charging equation even at quite low engine speeds.

The racing department of Joseph Lucas, as well as being specialists in fuel injection and specially tuned distributors for engines fitted with performance camshafts, also provide an excellent service for rally drivers with their supply of competition specification dynamo and alternators to special order. These are expensive, but worthwhile, as are some of the special components that they have developed over years of competition experience servicing the rallies of the world. Standard alloy cast dynamo end-brackets have been known to sheer thanks to the vibrations of a rally engine over many thousands of competition miles, so Lucas developed cast iron ones instead. They found too that the field coils inside a dynamo can become detached, so they incorporated ones cemented in place into their competition units. Then certain through bolts were found to come loose, so these were drilled and wired. Gradually many of these lessons learned in the exaggerated conditions of competition have been passed on to benefit the trouble-free service expectancy of standard components. Therefore, if an owner wants the best and is prepared to spend money and take time to achieve this, then such units will seem to be worthwhile. If he cannot afford the time or money, then a periodic overhaul or complete exchange of all his standard moving electrical components is prudent.

The best advice on wiring is to keep it as simple as possible. If the driver or crew members carry this work out themselves at least their understanding what goes where may turn out to be exceptionally useful during an event if something goes wrong electrically. If the work is carried out by somebody else, then one or more members of the crew must be able to understand what has been done, and, more important, how to fix it if anything goes wrong at a later date. All additional wiring on any rally car should be colour coded, preferably to the standard Lucas system. Also, a fuse board should be inserted into the additional wiring, so that all the extra accessories are individually controlled by a fuse and isolated in case something unfortunate happens. It is sensible to affix a card in place above a board with a reference of wire colour and fuse identification, to which a crew member can easily refer on the event itself.

All wire runs should be made plenty long enough to allow for movement. Grommets of course should be fitted wherever a wire or wires run through a panel. All joints should be soldered, or at least crimped with a proper crimping device, and new connections, with plastic covers where necessary, should be used.

It is perhaps best to decide in advance of fitting any individual wires what additional electrical items are going to be needed. All the wires should then be cut to length and tacked together at intervals with tape in accordance with the planned layout. It is amazing how often a layout will have to change during this operation. At least with all the wires out of the car, it is a relatively easy job to effect changes in wire position, colour, or length. The ends should all be bared in readiness for connections whilst they are completely accessible out of the car. Next, the mini-loom should be tightly bound with plastic or PVC insulating tape to prevent the wires from wandering, as well as keeping them entirely separate from the standard wiring. This separation helps to further isolate any trouble if this were ever to occur, as well as making it a much easier job to quickly move the extra wiring to a new car or bodyshell. Not that this should prove necessary all that frequently, we hope!

Once in place in the car, the auxiliary loom must be secured carefully in place with wiring clips at regular intervals. Although these can be fixed to the bodyshell with self-tapping screws, it is best, once sure that all the wires that are required have really been taken into account, to rivet the clips in place.

As far as the auxiliary fuse board is concerned, it will obviously help on an event if this can be reached by either crew member without their having to release their safety belts. Naturally spare fuses should be taped in place nearby.

On a rally car's electrical system, it is very wise to protect any switches if they are likely to be used a great deal, or in particular if they stand any chance of becoming overloaded, with relays. They are not difficult to wire into any circuit, though they should be securely mounted so that there is no possibility of them coming adrift and causing an electrical fire.

LIGHTS

The mounting of lamps is very much dependent on personal preference, as is the exact choice of lamps. But they must be really firmly mounted and, what is more, remain in this state for the duration of a rally. It is best if the frontal auxiliary lamps are fitted to a sturdily constructed lamp bracket, which, to be essentially practical, should be removable for daylight special stage events, as well as for ordinary road use. Despite this feature, when fitted the bar must be sufficiently foolproof, so that it cannot become too easily detached during an event. Brackets must result in the forward facing auxiliary lamps being within the legal minimum height ruling, as laid out by the Ministry of Transport in their current Vehicle Lighting Regulations. As these change periodically, the details of current legislation should be checked fairly regularly. Suffice it to say here, that extra lights whether they be fog, spot or driving lamps, must not be mounted too low down if they are to be used on public roads in conditions other than in fog or falling snow. Officially, the extra lamps must be operated in pairs, in that, in fog, two lamps must be used rather than just one and extra lamps must be symmetrically mounted, within a distance of sixteen inches of the outer edges of the vehicle, if they are to be used instead of headlamps at any time. The FIA's Group regulations must be studied too, if major events are contemplated, to ensure that a proposed lighting layout is going to comply.

If, as on a Mini, it may be necessary from time to time to be able to work on the area of a vehicle behind its radiator grille, then the lamp bracket, even if there is no intention by the owner to make it so that it is detachable, must be made so that it can at least swing out of the way for grille removal and access beyond. But whether fixed, swinging or detachable, the wires to the extra front lamps must be very well insulated with extra binding or be run within flexible conduit such as hose piping. Wires should be long enough so that they never become damaged through stretching. It is on the cards that the front of a rally car may become damaged at some time, so all wires leading to the lamps must be made so that they can accommodate any deformation in the area around the lights. Whether the extra lamps are intended to be detachable or not the wiring for each lamp must be easily separated for the roadside changing of an individual lamp, together with its immediate feed wire. Wherever the wires for the front lamps pass through an apron panel, the edge of each aperture must be covered with a grommet, loosely fitting around the cable to allow movement, so that no chafing of the wiring occurs. For a most efficient and neat job where the lamp and bar have to be detachable, a caravan or trailer electrical multi-pin-plug and socket makes a reliable connection, which will stand up to frequent usage. The best sort of plug and socket to obtain is the rubber covered variety, the socket side of which can be neatly mounted flush into the vehicle's front panel, so that when the plug is withdrawn, the lamps not being required, the socket can be sealed off from the elements with its own bung plug.

It may be that an owner will not want to go to the trouble of involving himself and his car with very much extra wiring, preferring to keep this to the absolute minimum. If this is the case, he may not want to go to the trouble of fitting an auxiliary fuse box in the cockpit, just running a feed direct down to the front lamps. This is preferable to pushing the live wire for the extra lamps through a dash-mounted switch. Ideally, to involve him with the minimum of expense and inconvenience, he should introduce in-line fuses into the combined feed line for all his additional front lamps as well as one for each lamp itself, so that any short circuit trouble can be isolated, thus causing the minimum of damage to any other wiring.

There are a mass of auxiliary lights on the market. However lamps should be chosen which are fitted with quartz-iodine or halogen bulbs. For ease of bulb replacement lamps with sealed beam light units should be avoided. The exact combination of lights is entirely dependent upon personal choice though there are two guiding rules. White light is more penetrating than amber, and the largest round lamps possible should be selected regardless of styling considerations. As for the type of lens and the formation in which lights should ideally be fitted, no two top rally drivers would agree. Under these circumstances, I feel the most usual selection is therefore the most relevant. This is for a pair of fog wide-beamed lenses as well as a pair of driving lenses. Actual spot lights went out of vogue when people started to fit headlamp units into fog/spot lamp bodies, so because of their limited, but concentrated, lighting result, they should be avoided. It is helpful if all the auxiliary lights at the front of a rally car are standardised for ease of interchanging parts.

If larger events are going to be entered then it might be sensible if the rallyist were to select his lamps from the ranges of manufacturers such as Cibie, who, being competition orientated, traditionally support competitors in the field by servicing their customers. However attractive some lamps may appear on discount or novelty, always choose lamps, the spares for which are abundantly available. This latter benefit is one very good reason for deciding on Lucas lights, for even in the wilds a wayside garage on a rally route might possibly be carrying spare lenses and bulbs for a popular range of lights upon its shelves.

In addition to an array of lamps across the front of any rally car it is sensible to make sure that the standard headlamps being augmented by the auxiliaries do their job properly. Light units should be changed if their reflectors become discoloured and their light output impaired.

There are numerous up-rating headlamp light units and bulb kits on the market, most of the leading lamp manu-

31 The best navigator's cockpit installation is usually the simplest. Here, without interfering with the standard equipment, an Escort Twin Cam has had a navigator's light; time of day clock; time elapsed on section clock; Halda Twinmaster, with two tripmeter windows, fitted under the cowling for anti-glare reasons on the navigator's side of the car. The driver has instant access to a simple set of switches controlling the extra, but basic, electrical equipment.

32 Adequate silencing, particularly for low-slung high-powered rally cars has become more of a problem in recent years due to increasingly severe maximum decibel output legislation. Silencers must be in first-class condition, well protected with skids, and even mounted across the rear of the vehicle to avoid possible damage on rough roads.

33 All sorts of experimental gadgets are used from time to time by the factory teams to cope with the problem of keeping headlamps clean and protected. On daylight sections, auxiliary lamps should be covered with stone-guards, whilst Perspex shields can be fitted across the headlamp apertures. Perhaps this installation is the ultimate, there being special wiping/washing equipment for the headlamp face.

facturers offering versions for popular sized apertures. These
may only change the standard type of bulbs for dipping quartz-
iodine ones of higher wattage. As I have said sealed beams
are never to be recommended for rallying, as it only needs a
lens to receive a crack from a flying stone for a complete unit
to become useless. For cars with just the conventional two
headlamps as standard, the very best iodine lamp conversion
available, albeit rather expensive, are those that embody two
reflectors in the one light. With these units, two iodine bulbs
can be illuminated at one time, both with their own reflector,
thus achieving twice the light output from the one light unit
on mainbeam. Another advantage with these units is that both
bulbs and reflectors are perfectly aligned to each other, there
being no compromise on filament location within the same
glass envelope, as would be the case with any conventional
dipping twin filament headlamp bulb. For four headlamp
systems, a complete set of iodine headlight units can be fitted,
so that all four lights are iodine on mainbeam, and only two
are left on for dipped beam. At least with light units fitted
with separate iodine bulbs, if the lens does become cracked,
the lamp still stays alight. One important point about quartz-
iodine or halogen bulbs is that very great care must be taken
when handling the bulbs themselves, so that no fingers touch
the surface of the bulbs' glass. On the longer events, spare
light units, as well as bulbs, should be taken along, stored
carefully on board the rally car, or preferably carried by the
service crew. If the equipment fitted is sophisticated, it may
be very difficult to obtain spares during an event, particularly
from the average countryside garage who should never be
expected to be able to supply from stock a rare Continental
light originally conceived solely with the rallyist in mind.

The rougher the event, or the more precious a set of lamps
are to a driver, the more careful he should be to cover over all
the forward facing lamp glasses with protective covers during
daylight running. It is best to use lamp covers that are relatively
expendable, as they have a nasty tendency of either falling
off or being purloined by the ' light fingered brigade '. I think
the best covers are those which show the outside world whether

K

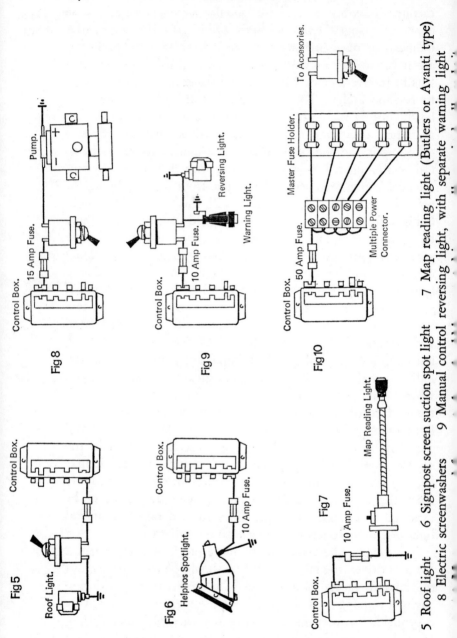

Fig 5
Control Box.
Roof Light.

Fig 6
Control Box.
Helphos Spotlight.
10 Amp Fuse.

Fig 8
Control Box.
15 Amp Fuse.
Pump.

Fig 9
Control Box.
10 Amp Fuse.
Reversing Light.
Warning Light.

Fig 10
Control Box.
50 Amp Fuse.
Multiple Power Connector.
Master Fuse Holder.
To Accesories.

Fig 7
Control Box.
10 Amp Fuse.
Map Reading Light.

5 Roof light   6 Signpost screen suction spot light   7 Map reading light (Butlers or Avanti type)
8 Electric screenwashers   9 Manual control reversing light, with separate warning light

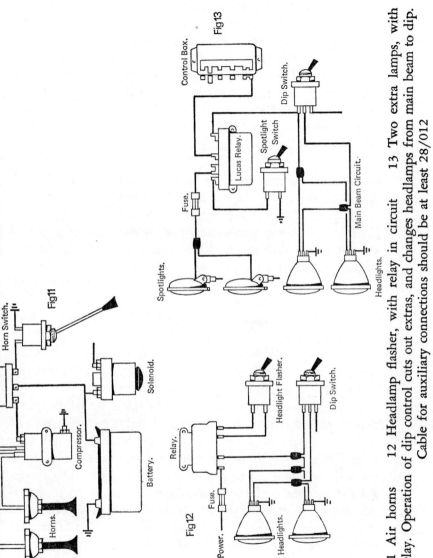

11 Air horns   12 Headlamp flasher, with relay in circuit   13 Two extra lamps, with relay. Operation of dip control cuts out extras, and changes headlamps from main beam to dip. Cable for auxiliary connections should be at least 28/012

the lamp has been left on or not through a small window. Cibie manufacture excellent semi-opaque plastic clip-over covers for their slim lamps, which are extremely easy to store inside the car when lamps need to be uncovered for nocturnal action, yet show a driver immediately if he has left any lights turned on at the front. For their larger lamps, including the famous Oscar fog and driving lamps, they market slatted covers, which can be left clipped to the front of these lamps, whether day or night, the light coming through onto the road all right, with the venetian blind ribbing stopping stones from smashing into the front of the lenses. Perspex covers work well too for all lamps, especially headlamps, though to prevent distortion of the light pattern intended by the lamp manufacturer, such covers should be as flat as possible. There are various clear covers on the market for headlamps, which by fairing in the light unit with the surrounding body section, claim improved streamlining, reduction of wind resistance and, usually a matter of taste, transformed appearance. Such covers do destroy a very vauable percentage of light output from the lights they shield, although they can be retained night and day. Perhaps the best feature of clear lamp covers is that light units are at least protected effectively from rocks flying up, a distinct possibility even from the wheels of the rally car itself. But on the other hand, Perspex covers do tend to become scratched very easily, and so their transparency rapidly deteriorates.

Although the legal requirements for reversing lamps decree that no reflectors must be fitted to such lights and the power of their bulbs must be kept down to something more akin to a fairy light, any rally driver who professes to take his sport seriously will continue to arm himself with a sufficiently power-ful light at the back, by whose light he can see to reverse— certainly a necessity at speed. Reversing lamps should be of the fog variety, so that a following car does not have to put up with any reflector dazzle, this being diffused sufficiently on a fog lamp, the lens of which will be fluted. They should never be mounted too low down either, as they will only stand more of a chance of becoming knocked out of action by lumps of scenery that might be thrown up by a rally car's rear wheels.

The back fixing fog lamp is perhaps the most suitable of all auxiliary lights for the job, as its mounting eliminates the need for a bracket.

It may be that the organisers will say in the regulations for a particular event that official Vehicle Lighting Regulations will be enforced under pain of penalty points. If this is the case, a return to the smaller and normal type of reversing lamp kit or standard lamp will have to be made. What is virtually certain is that most rally start scrutineers will check that all competitors have a fully operational reversing lamp warning-light fitted to their dashboard or a switch that is internally illuminated when the reversing lamp is turned on.

A map reading light is another basic item on any rallyist's electrical equipment. Depending on the installation, this may be best if it is a number-plate lamp mounted on the dash-board directly above where maps need to be read. On the other hand, it is more likely to be a case for a flexible map reading light, of which various lengths are manufactured, most being fitted with an adjustable hood covering or uncovering the bulb, according to the personal preference of the navigator. Spare bulbs should be carried by the navigator, or at least taped nearby. Also it may be found to be necessary to treat the flexible stalk for anti-glare if a driver complains that the reflection of chrome distracts him in the form of a ghost image upon the screen. This can be done either with matt black paint or by covering the stalk with black plastic insulation or bind-ing tape.

On road sections at night, where navigation may be very intense if no time is to be lost, then a socket should be fitted on the navigator's side of the car, so that he can plug in an illuminated map magnifier. Such a socket should be two-pin. It should also be of such a design that it is only possible for the plug to be plugged in the one way round. This prevents a possible short circuit if the magnifier's body is metal. On the subject of magnifiers the very best sort will have a variable resistance wired into it, or controlling the feed socket's power output, so that the navigator can dim the light down to the absolute minimum.

On certain cars it may be impractical to fit a reading light on the dashboard especially when rally seating has been added, possibly further away still from the dash. With such installations it might be better, rather than fitting a long flexible lamp which can very quickly start to sag, if a shorter flexible one is mounted above the navigator's door. This is very much more sensible than actually fitting such a lamp onto the door itself, with the obvious problem of wire fatigue, through constant hinging as the door is opened and closed.

To complete a rally car's lighting, if a car is to have everything, then lamps to illuminate the boot and underbonnet might well come in useful. But great care should be taken over the wiring of these, so that no chafing occurs. Extra sheathing of any wiring is essential and adequate clips too, it being far too dangerous if some object were to break loose in the boot and short out the wiring for the light. The bulbs of such lights should be well protected with wire or tough plastic guards, and the circuits fused as an essential precaution. Although the best types of lamp to use for this job are flexible map reading lights, particularly for underbonnet usage, number plate lamps are cheaper, and do not trail about to get in the way.

CONTROLS AND GADGETS

Also on matters electrical, it may be found preferable by a driver for his instrumentation, particularly the dials which may be crucial on an event, to be doubled up with warning lights. If a section on a rally becomes really taxing for the driver, and he becomes fully occupied steering the car between the trees as well as having to make frequent gearchanges, then warning lights are his answer. This is the case in the crowded high speed traffic of stock-car racing, where a driver does not have the time to read an instrument. The wires to these warning light bulbholders may simply be a matter of extending ones from the standard warning light cluster to new positions on the dashboard in eye-line with the driver. Complete new runs may be required which, if the case, should be incorporated into the auxiliary loom before it is finally fitted in place.

When working out the length of the extra wires on a rally car's electrical installation, the positions of the switches should all be moved as close to hand as possible, without being in the way of gearlever or steering-wheel. As it may be that somebody other than the driver will be driving a rally car from time to time, it is very helpful for anybody who is not totally familiar with the layout of the switchgear and what does what, if all the switches are labelled with ' Dynotape '. This is of especial value for when a strange co-driver is expected to drive a sleeping driver on a road section (if the driver is going to get any sleep that is!). If switches cannot be brought absolutely to hand, then extensions for the toggles can easily be rigged up with pieces of fuel tubing or proprietary switch extensions.

A golden rule of rally car dashboard planning is that it matters not what it all looks like. It must be functional and, above all else, everything should be very secure, so that nothing breaks adrift or rattles loose in the middle of an event. Operating a dashboard's controls should be only a matter of glance and feel. If a driver is to give himself a fair chance of doing well, there will be little time for anything more. Therefore headlamp flasher and air horns should all be simply a matter of a minute deflection of a micro-contact stalk switch, of which to avoid confusion there are various lengths on the market. It might be useful, especially where Continental rallying is envisaged, if the front passenger's side of the car is equipped with a horn control; preferably a horn push-button fitted to the floor. The best sort of overdrive controls are those combined gearlever knobs and overdrive switches, which once upon a time appeared on the Healey 3000 works cars, and now, in more modern form, have been adopted as original equipment by many vehicle manufacturers.

Other gadgetry, which should be considered before the owner commits himself to a final specification for his rally car, are a legion. Air horns are easy to fit and are a sensible addition to the standard equipment, it being best to choose horns with the more robust metal trumpets rather than plastic. The switch should of course always be protected from arcing itself into a permanently open or closed circuit by the inclusion of a relay into the accessory's wiring. The trumpets should not be mounted too low down at the front, as they tend to fill up with water so being rendered inoperative. Nor should they be fitted tucked away behind a panel, so that their hootings become so muffled that the advantage of fitting them in the first place is eradicated.

It is seldom that the standard screenwasher on any car will be up to rally conditions, either in volume of reservoir capacity or power of jet. Reservoirs should be fitted so that freezing of the contents will be as difficult as possible, preferably by fitting inside the cockpit itself. In this position, it is easier for a crew to keep a check on the level anyway. It is preferable if a plastic bottle is chosen, rather than a glass jar, for safety and durability in service reasons. At least, if it does freeze, a plastic container will not crack open. Another tip is to affix the reservoir top to the bottle itself with a small length of chain or wire, in the manner that the radiator and petrol caps have (it is hoped) already been modified. This avoids the top becoming lost after a hasty refill of the reservoir during an event, with the result that most of the fluid slops out onto the navigator's maps, pullover or sandwiches.

Two jets are more reliable than one. An ' On ', ' Stay on ', then ' Stay off ' type of switching is better in practice, than the more normal practice of wiring an electrical screenwasher through a button switch. This is because a driver may become too busy to hold onto the switch for a jet of water playing onto his screen, whilst seeking the wiper switch, changing gear, negotiating a hairpin, and putting out a cigarette—all at the same time! But this is really a personal decision. There are also conversions on the market to electrify manual screenjet installations. But, if more screenjet tubing has to be fitted, this must always be cut long enough to avoid pull-offs at ' T ' pieces, nozzles, as well as jar and pump motor outlets.

It might be as well, at this point, to say that there is no substitute for proper screenwasher additives. Household detergents can clog up impellers, motors, pumps, tubes and nozzles. Even in freezing conditions, great restraint should be exercised on not pouring vast amounts of anti-freeze into a screenwasher, the internal materials and mechanics of which may not be designed to be able to cope with the chemicals contained in the fluid.

Wiper arms and blades should be changed regularly. They do deteriorate rapidly enough anyway. Naturally, high speed arms and blades should be chosen, if these have not already been fitted. It may be found useful for the shiny metal surfaces of arms and blades to be carefully blacked out with matt black paint, so that no distraction is caused by their glinting the light from the heads and driving lamps back through the screen. But, if standard components are retained, then the spring tension of the arms must be sound and the lips of the blades not ragged, but knife-edged.

The most important thing about wiping equipment is that it should be in perfect condition. The wiper motor should be regularly exchanged for a factory reconditioned unit, or at least the brushes should be periodically replaced before they wear out. The same goes for wheel-boxes which should be free from excessive play. Particular attention should be spent on ensuring that the various nuts in the wiper linkage are kept tightened up, particularly the one that affixes the rack to the electrical motor, as this invariably seems to come undone. At least these days, the standard wiping equipment on most cars is entirely adequate for rallying. But even so, Lucas, for instance, market a whole range of two-speed wiper motors, which fit in place of single speed motors on several British cars. A high-speed racing wiper motor is ideally to be avoided because of the extremely short life expectancy of such ultra-special units.

There are various devices available which can be wired into the electrical circuit for screenwiper operation, either for controlling the speed of the motor electrically, or introducing a variable or fixed delay into the wiper operation. These are useful in slight drizzle or patchy fog, when leaving the wipers on, particularly with perfect arms and blades, would quickly overheat the motor, possibly causing premature failure. It must be emphasised that however laudible such electronic gadgetry is in principle and in operation, the wiring of such a device must be understood by the driver, so that he knows what to do in the event of anything going wrong. Such luxuries are in any case just more things to go wrong.

There was a time when most rally cars had electric heater bars, affixed by suction to the insides of front and rear screens, to demist them. These were often fitted in addition to the standard heater ducting. As the power and efficiency of demisting equipment, fitted as standard in most modern cars, has improved, so the need for extra equipment to combat deficiencies in this direction have been virtually eliminated. It can be helpful however to add a strip of Perspex along the lower edge of the inside of the windscreen, so that the demist airflow is directed more accurately onto the screen's surface. Also where there are cars with very steeply sloping rear screens, it can be safer if a demist panel is fitted. There are all sorts of adhesive ones, but best of all is one that has an electrical element built into it. Heated front/or rear screens, with the element built into the glass at the factory, are of course best of all, but these are rather expensive, and, if the events being entered do not warrant expenditure of this nature, then they must be considered a luxury. For winter rallies, a Triplex laminated screen, with an element built into it, should naturally be considered a necessity, because of possible presence of freezing fog—perhaps the most horrific hazard a rallyist might have to face in the pursuit of his sport.

Whilst dwelling on the electrical preparation and modifications, if special stage rallies are going to be entered, or if the noise in a particular car's cockpit is unusually high due to the proximity of intense mechanical activity, then an intercom ought to be included. These are extremely hard to come by. However, G. A. Stanley Palmer, the firm who market the Gemini tripmeter, do supply intercom sets to rallyists. Normally, such sets carry their own batteries and so are independent from the vehicle's electrical circuits. The ideal set-up will be for there to be a set of headphones for the driver and a throat microphone for the co-driver, two-way systems not being considered in the interests of crew compatibility, it being possible for there to be audible disagreement!

Any average speed device or tripmeter for the co-driver's side of the car should be internally illuminated. Any readings from such units must be discernible not only by the co-driver or navigator at night, but, ideally by the driver as well. Apart from having an extremely effective light, well shielded and possibly controlled by a rheostat, it can be additionally useful if a magnifier is rigged up in front of the instrument's window to make reading at night easier. On longer events, where one crew member may have to keep the car going alone whilst his partner has a sleep, the navigational machinery should perhaps be fitted to the centre of the cockpit so that legibility can be a simple matter from both sides of the car. Several cars on the London to Mexico event had taken this aspect of cockpit and electrical preparation one stage further by fitting their trip-meters in the middle of the dash onto swivelling brackets, so that either crew member could refer to the equipment without having to crane themselves in their belts towards the centre of the car. Apart from a rheostat into the illumination electrical circuit for all instruments, hooding of the top edges of all such equipment, so that no glare shines up to the screen and reflects back into the driver's eyes to distract him, must be considered if this is a problem. In any case, all the bezels of instruments and accessories in the cockpit must be carefully painted matt-black to prevent any ghost images shining on the screen. Such things as horn rings and the chrome on gearlevers can be most off-putting to a driver, particularly in fog, when his con-centration will already be taxed to the full. Steering wheels must be carefully chosen to avoid obtaining one whose spokes are highly polished. It is possible to obtain sports wheels, the alloy spokes of which have been ready anodised black for anti-glare reasons.

The placing of additional instruments is all very much a personal choice. There are auxiliary panels available for the most popular cars that are likely to be rallied. Development work has been carried out, in such cases, so that the panels are a straight-forward fitting exercise. However, when fitting extra instruments, it is better if a complete sub-panel, with all the dials and switches, is evolved for simplicity of servicing the car when it is actually on an event and time may be precious. The wiring should be made long enough for the panel to be removed sufficiently from its resting place for any of the instruments to be withdrawn if necessary, as well as for there to be sufficient access to the rear of the panel for wiring to be re-affixed to a switch back. An extras panel must be rigidly mounted, even if it has to be easily removable for there to be sufficient access to the rear of the panel for wiring and connections. It must be given a fair chance of staying reliable. The fixings for a panel should be firm therefore, but simple to detach. Self-tapping screws are all very well for a panel which is unlikely to be moved all that frequently, but with frequent usage, they do tend to rattle loose more often. Some sort of captive studs work best of all, using nuts fitted with wing grips, perhaps the same sort of accessories that racing cyclists use to lock their spoked wheels in place, but always with quick release in mind.

Instruments on sub-brackets, although often more convenient as the standard car's dashboard is disturbed less, do tend to shake about more. But if the vehicle is being entered in Group One for standard cars, then any additional equipment has to be definitely supplementary, so that the standard services are left undisturbed. It can sometimes be possible to update certain basic models, by obtaining the GT or sports model's dash assemblies. Often such an extra, being an item of production equipment, fits into the basic model perfectly.

Although a particular car may well have been fitted up with a roll-over protective set of hoops during the shell's construction, if any serious rallying is being done, then it is sensible to fit a roll-over bar, or preferably a complete cage, inside the cockpit. Wherever any of the bars pass near either crew member's head, sponge rubber should be bound in place as padding. Special care should be taken to ensure that roll-bar bolt ends do not point towards the occupants, as these can be extremely dangerous in the unfortunate event of an accident. Often proprietary roll-bar assemblies, particularly for rally applications, need spreader plates of a wider area to prevent these pulling through a shell floor or panel. Naturally, the bolt heads should be lowermost and the nuts and bolt threads uppermost when any part of a roll-cage is attached to a floor panel. This will avoid bolt threads becoming damaged when the underside of a car is dragged across rough ground, as may well turn out to be the case on any event on which a piece of rough track is used.

If the competitor plans to compete on the larger events anyway, a roll-cage will be compulsory. The material, fittings and design of an approved bar is important though, as it will have to comply with FIA regulations governing such things. This legislation even applies to Group I saloons on internationals. As a general rule, the safety cage should be made of two main hoops, one behind the front seats and one following the screen pillars. However, for practical reasons, the fitting of such a cage is made compulsory only for cars of which the weight declared on the FIA form of recognition, explained earlier, is above 1,200 kg. For cars under this weight, the screen hoop need not be fitted, but the general design has to follow the FIA Year Book's drawings. The material type and dimensions are another aspect that will be checked for compliance. The main hoop has to be as near to the roof as possible to limit its crushing in an inversion and it has to have a pair of back braces, ideally with a diagonal cross brace.

However amateur the participant's approach may be, he should never shun safety even though a roll-bar may well appear to be the ultimate in inconvenience and over-specialised equipment. Not only will it, together with both crew members always wearing safety belts, help to minimise the chances of personal injury to the occupants, but the bodyshell itself might well be saved from being written off, being held together basically by the bar.

Apart from choosing a steering wheel so that the spokes are free from glare, the rim of any steering wheel fitted to a rally car should be selected with safety in mind. It has to withstand considerable use, so should be fairly thick, well-padded, with some give so that road shocks can be minimised and blisters avoided. The best wheels are those whose spokes are fitted at their rim ends with thumb grips. It may be necessary to bind the sharp edges of the rims, so that a driver's thumbs do not become sore over a long event.

Although it is hardly necessary to go to the trouble of fitting a complete fire system along the lines of those fitted to most racing cars, with cylinders that can be activated from inside or outside the car manually, by inertia switch or heat sensing devices, a really decent-sized fire extinguisher must be carried in a rally car. Fires on rallies always seem to happen when an extinguisher is not being carried. Perhaps the best sort of extinguisher to purchase is one that, once activated, can at least be turned off when required, and not used up all at once. This should be fitted so that both crew members can reach it. In the event of a bad accident, knocking one crew member out of action, such accessibility of the extinguisher may turn out to be vital.

Also in the cockpit, pedal rubbers should be maintained in good condition, and replaced regularly if necessary. The pedals are so often overlooked even in supposedly the best prepared rally cars. The pads on many production cars are often not man-enough for severe rally usage, nor are they ideally positioned for toe heeling. So that the driving position and comfort is given the priority they deserve, it may be necessary to dismantle the pedals from the car, either cutting and re-welding, or bending them to achieve the desired pedal positions to suit the driver.

Carpets are seldom practical for rallying, being difficult to dry out quickly. Ideally, they should be replaced with rubber mats, or at least covered by them in the areas most likely to be affected by the heavy patter of a crew's muddy feet.

On certain models, experience may show that it is very helpful to cut hatches in the shell, so that specific servicing jobs can be carried out more speedily during an event. Such a case is the dry suspension Mini, especially if this has been fitted with an export petrol tank opposite the standard one. To make the task of re-attaching, replacing the top bushes, or replacing the rear shock absorbers, it has been found useful by Mini exponents for small hatches to be cut behind the rear seat back, so that the top shock absorber attachment nuts can be reached without the removal of either petrol tank being necessary. Particularly if it is possible for petrol to pour through such a hatch in the event of an accident, such servicing appertures should be fitted with miniature fluid and flame-proof doors. The edges of the hatches should also be well blunted to avoid a crew or service crew member receiving a cut hand on sharp metal edges.

Provision should be made in any cockpit for either crew member to reach a torch, it being better for at least two torches or lanterns to be taken along on a rally. A first aid kit should be carried too. And rags and hand cleanser may seem unnecessary, but do prove to be a boon after work has had to be done by either crew member. Oil and muck on the steering wheel or maps is never conducive to accuracy by either crew member.

WHAT TO TAKE WITH YOU

There should be a place for everything taken along. Time cannot be wasted having to rummage amongst piles of clothing, sandwiches, tools and spares for a vital item of equipment to be located in a hurry. On a special stage event, canvas or stout cardboard bins ought to be fitted into the rear of the cockpit, so that crew members' crash helmets can be safely transported with the minimum of damage between special stages. A tool roll, or a series of pockets, can be most usefully employed attached to the back of the rear seat, so that the rule of ' a place for everything, and everything in its place ' can be conscientiously adhered to. Expandable elasticated thongs, as used by scooterists to affix luggage onto their carriers, can be most usefully employed in quantity in any rally car, so that everything can be held in place and prevented from damaging itself, surrounding objects, the vehicle, or even the crew members.

It is impossible to generalise on which item of equipment should be stored in the cockpit, and which in the boot. It all depends on the type of vehicle being used and indeed the type of event being entered. I have always found that both the jack, handle, and the wheelbrace should most certainly be carried in the cockpit, securely stowed, and immediately accessible to either crew member. I have also found that the tools should be best stored in the cockpit as well, so no time is wasted rummaging in the boot.

If there is a back window ledge, all sorts of spares of a lighter nature, such as a spare fanbelt, bulbs, contact set, hoses and gaskets can be taped in place ready for instant service. Whereas, in the boot, such heavier spares as halfshafts, drive couplings, alternator, and suspension components are more at home. Great care should be taken so that items stored in the boot, along with the spare wheels, do not chafe or puncture the wiring, battery or petrol tanks.

No rally cockpit is complete without there being the inevitable rolls of wire and tape, as well as a selection of nuts and bolts, all likely to be useful in the event of something requiring patching up in action.

Boot and cockpit content preparation is so often a last minute panic affair, usually involving both crew members hurling all manner of objects that either of them consider may come in useful during an event. The boot and interior's contents should be just as carefully planned and prepared as the car itself. Heavy spares ought to be stowed as low as possible. Spare wheels should be instantly accessible, yet stored in such a way as to be unlikely to break adrift. Spare petrol, either in cans or proper fuel bags, should be taken along. Also spare oil and water are vital, though the containers for these various fluids must be selected so that there is no likelihood of a mistake being made in the dark, with the result that water is added to oil or petrol is poured into a radiator. I once lost a certain class win on the Welsh International, when some well-meaning helper added a gallon of water to my petrol. It was dark, pouring with rain and both water and petrol were in similar unmarked oil cans! As a general rule, I would advise petrol to be carried in red painted metal containers, water in clear plastic bottles and oil in the maker's containers. On the subject of oil, it is always better to take along several small tins, rather than large gallon containers, as the smaller quantities are so much easier to pour into an engine without spillage in the dark. The screw-tops on such tins are a much

34 Competitors must be able to see their instruments without taking their eyes too far from the road ahead. This Imp has its rev counter right in line, all its switches labelled clearly, and a large warning light if the oil pressure were to fail in the middle of a hectic Special Stage. The navigator is confronted with basic equipment, like a large illuminated clock with secondhand and a single tripmeter.

35 Bonnets and boots should be secured in place for safety purposes with auxiliary and leather straps. Also shown on the front of this Mini is a caravan towing plug and socket, which has been usefully employed to make the feed to the additional lighting on the front end efficiently detachable.

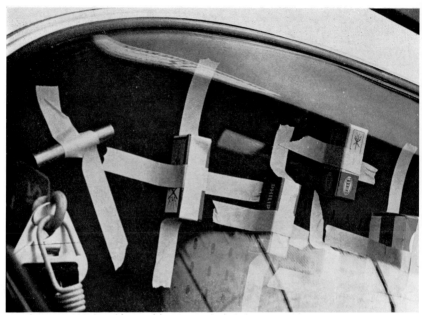

36   The inevitable but necessary loose spares should not be stored in inaccessible parts of the car. A good idea is to lay them out on the back ledge with tape.

37   Naturally spare topping up fluids should be taken along, such as oil, water, brake fluid, back axle oil, and spare petrol. There should be no confusion over which liquid is in which container. They must be securely stowed, preferably with elastic straps.

safer bet than tins that have been sealed with strips of foil, or whose contents are contained by milk bottle tops.

It is difficult to decide where to stop when emptying the contents of a garage into the rally car before it moves off to the start of an event. Certainly a tow rope of ample length, with stout hooks should be considered a must. The vehicle should ideally have an eyelet fixed onto each corner, so that whichever corner is nearer the edge, over which the rally car has had the misfortune to have travelled, it can have at least a chance at being retrieved. If the event is likely to be particularly muddy or cursed with thick snow, then such colourful equipment as a winch, chains, boards to put under the driving wheels to gain traction, and the classic spade, preferably portable, should be included. It can also be most helpful to carry a thin, but stout, square of board. This does not take up much room, yet can be most useful to place under the jack if a wheel change has to be made on soft ground. It spreads the weight of the jacked-up vehicle over a wider area of mud, so preventing the jack from sinking into the ground. It might be an idea instead, to weld a spreader plate onto the base of the jack itself.

Although slightly pessimistic, no rally car's boot preparation is complete without the inclusion of a crowbar, as well as a hacksaw. If a wing is pushed back onto a wheel, a quick leverage session with such a bar and cutting torn metal out of the way, if necessary, can make a rally car mobile again within seconds instead of such an incident putting the car out of action, until a fully equipped breakdown truck, at enormous expense, has to be summoned in the morning.

The boot lid itself, even if it is stoutly secured with a standard catch, should be held shut by thongs instead. A boot that is held shut by a key-operated mechanism must be converted, so that either crew member can gain access to its contents immediately, without having to remember who has the key. Rubber thongs are so much better anyway for holding hinging panels shut, as in the unfortunate event of an accident, they can accommodate any distortion as well.

L

6 The Organisers

It may be that a competitor will never want to be an organiser. It may be that competing is all that will ever really matter to him in his sport of rallying. On the other hand, there will be countless enthusiasts to whom marshalling is the total extent of their participation. Being on the organising side of an event is, indeed, the very best way for anybody to see for themselves what is really involved at the minimum of expense.

This part of the book therefore, has a twofold purpose; to lay out the system that has to be adhered to by any club or clubman who wants to put on a rally, examining the various roles of the personnel involved; and to give competitors the benefit of an insight into what goes on behind the scenes on every event, so that their understanding of the workings of their sport becomes more complete. For organising a rally under the legal requirements now in force in Great Britain is no easy matter any more. It is such a gargantuan task of paper-work that many clubs cry off before they ever present their ideas to the RAC Motor Sport Division. Such is the effectiveness of trying to limit the number of times interesting roads are used on rallies these days, that out of over 1,300 suggested rally routes submitted for approval by RAC affiliated motor clubs in 1970, only 750 reached fruition.

THE RULES

Some explanation of the rules governing motor sport involving competitors using the public highway must here be in order before progressing further. For there is not only the RAC to consider nowadays but the Ministry of Transport itself. A rally is defined as being a competition, of which the main part of the route is over highways, and in which marking for maintaining a time schedule forms a substantial part of the competition. Such a rally may include tests of course.

Every rally is subject to these Motor Vehicles (Competitions and Trials) Regulations made by the Secretary of State and the Ministry of Transport. Their authorisation procedure must therefore be followed by all who wish to run a rally. These extracts from the MOT's regulations for the authorisation of events on the public highway may prove to be of interest at this point.

' The Motor Vehicles (Competitions and Trials) Regulations 1969 require that every event which utilises the Public Highway be subject to authorisation and bound by the standing conditions of these regulations. The Ministry of Transport has appointed the Royal Automobile Club as the controlling agency on its behalf to undertake authorisation.

' The regulations require that all events, with the exception of those detailed below, are authorised by the RAC. Applications for such authorisations to be received a maximum of six calendar months and a minimum of two calendar months prior to the proposed date of the event. Below is a list of the events which are authorised automatically, but it must be noted that it is still necessary for all events to comply with the standing conditions specified in the regulations :

(a) An event in which the total number of vehicles driven by the competitors does not exceed twelve, being an event no part of which takes place within eight days of any part of any other event in which the total number of vehicles driven by the competitors does not exceed twelve and where either the other event has the same promoter or the promoters of both events are members of the same club in connection with which the events are promoted.

(b) An event in which no merit is attached to completing the event with the lowest mileage and in which, as respects such part of the events as is held on the Public Highway, there are no performance tests and no route, and competitors are not timed or required to visit the same places, except that they may be required to finish at the same place by a specified time.

(c) An event in which, as respects such part of the event as is held on a Public Highway, merit attaches to a competitor's performance only in relation to good behaviour and compliance with the Highway Code.

(d) An event in which all competitors are members of the armed forces of the Crown and which is designed solely for the purposes of their service training.

'Whilst authorisation for the above type of event is given automatically, it is suggested that the local police are advised that such an event is being organised in order that minimum inconvenience can be ensured whilst the event is in progress.

'Application forms for the authorisation for any other type of event are available from the Motor Sport Division and it is normally suggested that organisers submit their route application as far in advance as possible, for example up to a maximum of six months prior to the proposed date of the event. Under the regulations, the RAC is required to permit only a certain number of events on a road at any particular time and it may therefore be necessary to withhold permission, or to suggest an alternative date or alternative section of the route.

'In its recommendations for the Control of Motor Rallies, the Chesham Committee did advise that no cost should be borne by the general taxpayer for the provision of this authorisation procedure. Therefore, any event which has to be authorised through the controlling agency is subject to a basic fee of £5, with an additional fee of £3 for every fifty miles of highway that are used. It is not necessary to forward the fee on first application as charges are advised during the course of authorisation.

'(Copies of the Road Traffic Motor Vehicles (Competitions and Trials) Regulations 1969, price 10p, reference number 1969 414, and the Report of the Motor Rallies Advisory Committee, entitled Control of Motor Rallies, price 12½p, are available from Her Majesty's Stationery Office).'

Also for RAC recognised clubs using the public highway, the following extracts are salient.

' The Royal Automobile Club is also the controlling body of motor sport in Great Britain. All its regulations and requirements are included in two publications—the RAC General Competition Rules and the RAC Motor Sport Year Book, both of which are available from their Motor Sport Division at 40p each plus 5p each postage and packing.

' When an RAC recognised club makes application to the MOT controlling agency, at the RAC, for permission to utilise the Public Highway for an event, it should be noted that this does not absolve the club of the need to make application for an RAC permit. This application should be submitted in the normal manner for whatever type of event is being planned and should be not less than six weeks prior to the date of the event. This permit will not, however, actually be issued until confirmation is received of any amendments that the RAC may have requested and until such confirmation has been received that the event has MOT authorisation.

' In providing an RAC Permit for this event, recognised clubs are provided with free legal liability insurance for any event which does not utilise special stages—a third party legal liability indemnity amount of £100,000 for the promoters is provided in the club's annual recognition fee. Any contractual or third party insurance premiums for other events will be invoiced on application.'

In addition, the RAC have made arrangements for competitors to be able to organise personal cover when taking part in rallies, often difficult with ordinary insurance policies.

' A market is available through the RAC's official brokers, Messrs C. T. Bowring & Muir Beddall (Home) Ltd, The Bowring Building, Tower Place, London, EC3, to provide the necessary Road Traffic Act cover for competitive events taking place on the Public Highway and it is advised that this company is contacted for details.'

Any motor club might fancy the glamorous big-time of using

tracts of Forestry Commission property on their event. To do this, they must receive permission from the RAC. This is not easy, as there are a great many safety rules to be met before permission is granted. Anyway, most small and medium sized motor clubs would find the considerable charges involved per competitor mile would prohibit using these roads, which of course, form the basis of sorting out competitors in Great Britain's premier event, the RAC Rally. The rule for all motor clubs is that permission must be obtained from the landowner if they ever intend to route competitors on any private tracks.

If anyone wants to organise a rally therefore, the procedure is for it first of all to be decided when they may want to hold the event and what sort of event they envisage it to be. The basic budget, that will govern the setting-up of an event, will have to be worked out even before this by that event's founders. The format of whether an event will be all stages, all road sections, or a combination of the two, will have to be determined too. Organisers must also have some idea of the percentage of rough and smooth roads they have in mind, as well as how many competitors they anticipate will enter.

All these pre-decisions on planning that are necessary before authorisation is sought will either be the responsibility of the motor club committee or certain key members of the event's organising sub-committee. It may be that only one person will be involved in these initial decisions, either the eventual Secretary of the Meeting or the Clerk of the Course. The next step is for the event's officials to be appointed within the motor club. One person will have to be in charge right from the start of the planning, usually this will be the Clerk of the Course. Both he and the Secretary of the Meeting are required by the RAC to be named fairly early on during an event's formative stages. In fact most of the initial graft can be undertaken by this pair until much nearer the event. The next member to join such an action committee should ideally be the Chief Marshal, who may be required, in addition, to double up as the event's Public Relations Officer.

The Clerk of the Course needs first to complete a basic route, according to the pre-planning and the sort of geography that has been decided as being suitable for the scene of the event. Often this basic route is drawn up after consultation by the club with its regional association's rally committee; such a body will have the best idea of knowing what is happening on its region's territory rally-wise, and on which weekends. Such discussions do save organisers from having their route turned down straight away by the RAC, due to an already planned regional clash. Whilst drafting out this approximate route, an organiser ought to refer constantly to the current RAC ' Black Spot ' list, which is updated regularly in the RAC Motor Sport News, sent automatically to competition licence holders. Most Associations will also hold their own ' Grey Spot ' list, where opposition to rallying by local inhabitants has been discovered by previous events. Reference should also be made to this in the interests of good public relations for rallying in any area. Such relevant discussions ought ideally to be made at least seven or eight months before an event. In addition to working out where the route can go, avoiding the ' Black ' and ' Grey Spots ' on the map, any organisers worth their salt will next go out to discover whether the intended route is passable, or not, in reality. For all sorts of things can happen to a stretch of road since the map was made and Organisers have had their plans upset by anything from Motorway excavations across their intended route, road closures and land slides to discovering that a large slice of their route has been submerged after some valley has been flooded for a hydro-electric scheme. What might look on the map as if it might be a pleasantly deserted stretch of road skirting a town, can often turn out to be ' not-as-map ', being straight through the middle of a recently constructed housing estate—hardly ideal territory for the passage of a fleet of rally cars in the middle of the night.

The two forms organisers need to fill in are the MOT's E 404 ' Application for authorisation of a motoring event on the Public Highway ', which is usefully supplied to organisers by the RAC with an E 405 ' Notes for guidance on the completion of form E 404 ', and their own ' Application for a rally permit '. When submitting their route, as well as filling in these forms, it is essential for organisers to refer to the MOT's

Regulations themselves, with particular reference to the siting of control points, in that these must be situated at least five hundred yards from any occupied dwelling place, unless written permission has been obtained from the affected householder.

The Start and Finish points must be chosen so that they are fully capable of accommodating the number of competitors, marshals and spectators who are likely to turn up. The Start must have sufficient room available for competitors to be able to sign on and complete their documentation without over-crowding. There must be adequate room for scrutineering of the competing cars to be carried out, as well as all the com-petitors to be parked so that they do not have to be continually moved forward from one spot to another, as their start times become due. There should be adequate refreshment facilities organised with the Start and Finish locations, at prices the competitors can afford, and at the unusual hours they are likely to require them. The opening and closing times of such venues must be discovered by organisers, and altered to fit in with the timing of the rally if necessary. Most garage and hotel pro-prietors will be found to be most co-operative on this point, as the increase of their takings usually compensates them hand-somely for any inconvenience caused to their routine by the passage of a rally. Conversely, any hotelier or garage owner will not be happy to see rallyists again if an alteration is made to the route or timing to affect any special arrangements he may have made as far as laying on extra catering and staffing arrangements; the organisers should inform any hotelier or garage owner if alterations are made.

When a route is submitted, it is often impossible to avoid the use of the same piece of road on more than one occasion during an event, or indeed, in both directions, especially if an excess of ' Black Spots ' border the only route possible on part of a map. This is permitted, even both ways, on the way out of tight territory to a rest halt or special stage, but these parts of the route will naturally be most carefully checked by the RAC.

With all the forms completed, two copies of the intended route from OS one inch to the mile maps have to be submitted for the RAC to offer up this suggested route against their master set of maps, on which they keep a copy of every approved rally route for the whole of Great Britain. This tracing has to indicate clearly the route itself, the direction of travel planned for competitors, the times on and off the various maps, as well as the locations of all the controls. The route is then processed by the RAC to ensure that there is no duplication, either on the same night, or indeed within the stipulated period, so that the rationing of roads most likely to be required for regular rally use is strictly observed. If the event is being held in daylight, or the road requested is likely to be used in daylight, then no other event must have covered the same stretch of road within 14 days. At night the regulations are stiffer, for there must be no duplication of a piece of road being used within 28 days.

The final approved tracing, or rather one copy of it, will then be despatched to the relevant police forces concerned. However, if there are clashes, then the RAC will do their best to re-route up to ten per cent of an organiser's route to avoid a clash. Such a re-route will not utilise any white roads, because of it being impossible, from an office, to be absolutely certain that the tracks chosen might turn out, in fact, to be suitable for the passage of a rally. Main roads are exempt from the rationing rules, but even with these, the RAC does not like approving their use by any organiser within a week of another event.

The RAC also notify organisers of all the ' Black Spots ' near any route, so that they can, in turn, warn all competitors of their existence. Organisers can, with this information, deploy their marshals to any of these ' Black Spots ', especially if it is possible for the rally competitors to take a short cut through one.

With tracings a certain amount of to-ing and fro-ing is usually necessary, particularly on the more popular rally maps, until a route is finalised, organisers being given the opportunity of putting forward replacement controls for those that might have had to be scrubbed due to an RAC re-route. Any tracing amendments of course, have to be forwarded to the police for approval and information. Finally, once everything has been agreed over a route between the police, RAC and the motor club concerned, the club pays the MOT fee via the RAC, as well as sending the RAC its own fee. The particular rally is then on the road legally, having been given its permit to prove it.

SECRETARY OF THE MEETING

The Secretary is totally in charge of all the paperwork. He should have specific responsibility for filling in the forms for the RAC and compiling the event's regulations. The contents of these regulations should be based upon a set of master ones, laid out in the RAC's Year Book, or ' Blue Book ' as most people refer to it. The introduction will of course be different, and should tell the intending competitor what is in store for him, if he were to enter the rally. Then the awards should all be listed out, so the doubting competitor can finally be persuaded to take part. To help pay for the cost of printing a pile of regulations, it is the Secretary's job to attempt to muster up some advertising from those who might be interested in taking space in the regulations, or, best of all, sponsoring the whole event. A sponsor may meet many of the costs, such as paying for the print and production costs of all the paper-work involved, as well as even putting up silverware and prize money.

It may be found preferable in the compilation of the regula-tions for the Secretary to approach one of the concerns, who have specialised in the business of offering organisers a com-plete service—a package deal—whereby they print the regula-tions and approach advertisers on the organiser's behalf. Using such people, an organiser can on most occasions reduce his costs and possibly even have his regulations printed for noth-ing if the advertisers are attracted to the proposition of ad-vertising in a particular set of regulations in sufficient quantity. As these firms are professionals, regulations produced in their studios usually look more professional than offerings that are more of a do-it-yourself nature.

The Secretary will need to approach Stewards to find out whether they are available at the time of the event for duty.

On a closed to one club event, only a Steward for that club will be required. On an event where participation is restricted to various specified clubs, then a Steward will need to be appointed to represent the interests of the invited clubs' members. On an event of higher status, a Steward will need to be organised on behalf of the RAC as well. These various processes of regulation compilation should normally be commenced whilst the rally is being passed through the official authorisation machinery, so that some time might be saved.

It is not an RAC requirement for a RAC Scrutineer to be present for a rally, but a suitable person must be appointed by the organisers to carry out the routine tasks of checking that cars comply with the basic legal requirements at the start. The sort of checks such an official should be responsible for are on horns, wipers, indicators, brake lights, all auxiliary lights being over-ridden by the dipswitch, a warning lamp being operative when reversing lights are in use, and an exhaust system that silences effectively. After such start duties, he should then be responsible for organising the two obligatory *en route* noise checks with a decibel meter. It is also an RAC stipulation, that the findings of these checks should be made known to the competitors in the results. So, the communication of the findings of such checks will be another responsibility of the Scrutineer.

The Secretary, particularly on larger events, will appoint a Rally Timekeeper. Such an official is required anyway on any section of an event, which has to be timed to less than a minute, as is the case at the end of selective or special stage. If there is just going to be the special test, as a tie decider, then the Rally Timekeeper will be responsible for the timekeeping on that test, or, in the case of a whole series of tests, he will be in charge of delegating his timing duties amongst the marshals at the start and finish points of each test.

The Secretary is also responsible for the appointment of a Results Team Leader. It is best if he and helpers are fresh for this job and should not be recruited from those who might have already been marshalling all night. It is often possible to use for this job those who have worked at the start control of an all night event. For then, they can transport themselves straight to the finish, so that they can have some sleep, before having to work out the results.

On the subject of results, it is very important for any organiser to evolve a system of master sheets from the control points, as well as the actual competitors' time cards, which will make the Results Team's job a relatively speedy and foolproof one. The exact system of working out the results must be completely clear before the event starts, as competitors like to be given the results as soon as possible after they reach the finish. Advance arrangements must be made for all master time sheets from control point marshals who are not journeying to the finish, to be phoned in to the Results Team there. It might be useful for sector marshals to do the job of gathering up all the time sheets, at the same time as they close the course.

Another very vital task, that any rally Secretary has to undertake, is to do all the ' Thank Yous ' to the various landowners, sponsors and police forces, who might have been inconvenienced by the passing of the rally. Such a little thing helps greatly when the time comes round for the next rally, and permission is sought again.

Knowing to whom regulations should be sent is important, if the costs of mailing are to be limited, so that the distribution of the regulations is at its most effective. Most associations of motor clubs have a rally championship of their own, so such a championship's Secretary will have a list of rally competitors throughout that association's area. If the event is a restricted one, then contact ought to be made by the rally Secretary to the various editors of the invited clubs' news letters, so that rallying members of the various clubs can read all about the rally's existence. It might also be found helpful to place an advertisement in the enthusiast press, telling enthusiasts which clubs are invited and to whom application may be made for regulations to be sent. This expenditure will depend of course on the budget as well as the funds available.

All entries received by the Secretary should be acknowledged with a postcard, either saying that it has been accepted, put on the reserve list, refused, or held in abeyance until a later date when the applicant will be informed one way or the other. Entries can be handled by him either on the ' first-come first-served ' basis, or by waiting until a closing date is passed, before selecting the final entry list by seeding from those entries received, until the total allowed is reached. Especially for events that count towards some championship or other, it may prove best, if the first twenty places on the road are reserved for regular top ranking championship entrants. From then on the entry is selected on a ' first-come first-served ' basis.

The Secretary must ensure that all competitors receive a set of final instructions from the organisers. These should inform the entrant of his starting number and the time he has to report to the start for documentation and scrutineering, together with the points that will be scrutineered. It is helpful if a small sketch map of the layout of the start control is given to each competitor so that he will know when he arrives, where he should report for each stage of the start procedure. With these instructions, the Secretary is well advised to include all the Quiet Zones with which competitors will be required to comply, as well as all the ' Black Spots ', in which entry by competitors will be forbidden on pain of exclusion from the results. This will at least give all the navigators plenty of time to add this important information to their maps before the event.

Afterwards, the Secretary should gather up the Stewards' reports, or make sure that these are despatched to the RAC as soon as possible. A copy of all the paperwork, a route card and the results should all be sent to the RAC as well.

CHIEF MARSHAL

Along with the Clerk of the Course and the Secretary of the Meeting, the Chief Marshal should go out to check the course for himself. It is his job to inform the marshals individually, or in groups, where they should go. This can be done in a variety of ways : by post; in conjunction with the Secretary; by telephone; or by meetings prior to the event with prospective marshals. Two things are involved, the place and the time the marshalling has to be done. In the regulations for the event there should be a form for those who may be interested in marshalling to register.

He should prepare a master list giving him, at a glance, what time each control point should be manned, as well as a comprehensive location description. He should always have a reserve plan of coverage worked out for all the points, just in case a marshal does not turn up at his point when he should do.

A set of marshals' instructions should be compiled by the Chief Marshal, in conjunction with the Secretary. These should have a place left for the map references, and the times peculiar to each marshal crew. All the telephone numbers relevant to the running of the event should be included in these instructions, so that, at any time, a marshal knows who to phone and when, if anything goes wrong that might prevent him from meeting the time schedule expected of him by the organisers.

The Chief Marshal should deploy his marshals according to their experience, with the seasoned campaigners being seconded to the parts of the route that are expected by the Clerk of the Course to lose competitors time, and particularly to man the points at the end of any especially tight sections. Novices to marshalling should be despatched to look after passage checks, where no timing is involved. Instructions ought to tell marshals not only when and where they have to be, but also what they should take with them, such as clocks, torches, blankets and an umbrella.

The Chief Marshal should also make sure all his marshals understand the timing system being used on the event. A sample set of paperwork should be given to each one, so that, when a competitor does arrive at his control point, the marshal knows what all the paperwork is about.

In addition to a map reference for the control point, the Chief Marshal should give marshals a small sketch map, so that there is absolutely no doubt in each marshal's mind as to the exact place he should man. This is a particularly useful safeguard if nobody is going to be covering the route before the competitors arrive, to check that each marshal is in the right place. This small diagram should include any gateways if applicable, as well as the basic directions of the nearest town or village so that the novice can tie up the sketch with the map more easily, place names being possibly more comprehendable to the newcomer than just map reference numbers. Permanent signs or painted crosses in the roadway may seem ideal to inform the marshal of the point at which he should position himself, but will be most unpopular with the residents, as well as the local authorities. Anyway such unofficial semi-permanent road marking is illegal.

The Chief Marshal should make sure that all his marshals standardise on the siting of their controls, so that the competitor quickly knows what to expect. Ideally, all controls should be clearly evident with a board or flag, the same distance in advance of the point up the route, as well as another actually at the point itself. It may be possible for the colour of the boards or flags to differ, according to whether the marshal's point is timed, or merely a passage one. The marking of controls must be consistent throughout the event, as well as for the side of the car the marshals should be standing in relation to the competitors—this preferably ought to be standardised for the navigator's side.

As well as being the co-ordinating force behind any group of marshals, the Chief Marshal may also man a key control himself. Or he may open the route with the Clerk of the Course, either in the same car, or following in a reserve. He can even delegate his route duties, or parts of them, to sector marshals. He should organise reserves into a convoy if he is involved in the course opening, and should carry with him spare sets of paperwork, just in case one of the control points has mislaid their time sheets or cards, if the system being used is for the marshal to hand a time card out to each competitor.

Finally, he should make it his job to personally thank all the marshals for their labours, make sure that they all receive results, and that, if at all possible within the event's budget, organise and distribute free or part-paid breakfast tickets without anybody being left out.

MARSHALS

One of the first essentials of any marshal is for his car to be reliable. If this is not so, then a complete event can be upset by his not arriving at a control point. Marshals should be prepared to be self-sufficient as far as refreshments are concerned, for whilst competitors are able to make the most of catering facilities at official halts, the marshals might have to be moving to their next control point, or waiting halfway up a mountain for the competitors to arrive. So hot soup, food, flasks of tea or coffee should be taken along by any well prepared marshal's crew.

As a marshal crew's route will usually run across country, and so might not coincide with petrol arrangements that might have been made specially to cope with the demands of rally crews during an all night event, when garages will otherwise be closed up, adequate petrol should be carried so that the crew can fuel itself.

Clothing for any marshals must be warm, windproof and waterproof as hanging about outside facing the elements, is almost certain to be the case. The obvious umbrella should be taken along as well.

As many marshals do this to find out all about the sport, before taking part themselves, then it will be found to be excellent practice for mini-rallying in that a route between one or more points will often have to be followed to time. The car's lights will have to be suitably powerful for this job. The battery will have to be in extremely good condition if the engine is going to be restartable after a long spell at the roadside has occurred. Apart from extra lights, it will be found to be essential, if much marshalling is to be done, for the car to be progressively fitted up with most of the other items of rally equipment, with particular emphasis on a map reading light, and possibly a sumpguard.

The minimum of people who ought to make up each marshal crew is two with, once the cars start arriving, one staying inside the cockpit, keeping the master record sheet in perfect order and possibly being in charge of the clock as well if the competitors do not all want to refer to it for themselves; whilst the other less fortunate crew member will have to stay out in the weather, to either mark competitors' road books actually inside each cockpit, to pass the books into his companion in the marshal's car for stamping up, or to pass a pre-prepared time card from his companion to each competitor as they arrive.

Marshals should equip themselves with more than one torch, as well as a supply of coloured pens and biros. Coloured biro is less easy for any competitor to alter! Ink or felt tipped pens, however, should not be used, as the possibility of ink smudging or being water soluble would be too great. A stopwatch board ought to be taken along too, as this makes the most manageable board upon which to write. The marshal must be completely adept at reading the watch, whether this is one issued to each crew by the Chief Marshal, or a sealed watch handed out at each control by each navigator in turn. Timing must be completely fair and consistent for every car. Marshals must decide whether they clock each rally car on sight, or when it actually comes to a stop at the control. In the same way as timing must be totally fair, marshals must be very firm with any navigators who may try to shout up the time they require, rather than the actual time, if this is likely to be later. In short, each marshal's crew must be in charge of the point it is manning. Where any alteration has to be made to any time sheet or road book, if ever a mistake is made, such alterations must be endorsed by a marshal's signature. To avoid any cheating, this should be a full length signature and not just initials.

CLERK OF THE COURSE

The Clerk of the Course is in overall charge of any event. And it is he who has to have the responsibility if anything were to go wrong—especially afterwards, in front of the RAC. Once the route has been agreed, the locations of controls known, it is the C of C who must set the target times for the sections of the route, always remembering that the average speed must not exceed 30 mph, or rather must not be seen to do so!

He is responsible for the design of the documentation with particular reference to the time sheets and/or cards, in conjunction with the results team leader. He should know how and when paperwork is to be handed out to the Chief Marshal for distribution to the marshals, as well as to the competitors them-

M

selves. The production of all the cards and timing paperwork, as well as the overall timing, is all part of his job.

Perhaps the most glamourous part of his job is the opening of the route itself on the night. But it is also important to organise others into closing it after the rally has gone through, so that any unfortunates who have broken down along the way, do not become stranded in the wilderness, and that a report of any damage to anybody's walls or hedges can be verified or contested. This closing of courses is very rarely carried out, yet is so important. As already suggested, a course closer can also collect the master time sheets from each control, acting as a dismissing authority for all the marshals.

He should naturally have covered the whole route which he is controlling. It is also wise, if he is to request an experienced rally crew, known by him not to be taking part in the event itself, to cover the route to try out the timing imposed by him on the sections. Also all the other organising officials' functions are his responsibility. If anything goes wrong at all with the event, then the buck stops at the Clerk of the Course.

PUBLIC RELATIONS

One of the most important aspects of organising a rally has become Public Relations. The RAC likes to see this carried out, as informing the public of what is to occur is one of the best ways to cut down the number of complaints afterwards.

Firstly, one member of the organising team must be made PR. Then the budget of the event must be consulted to see which way the PR work can be done within the financial framework decided in advance by the event's organisers. At the very least, notes through householders' doors that line the route must be carried out, certainly known to be useful to the cause of smooth relations with the public. But individual calls on each householder in person are best of all. However, it is possible for him to delegate the often considerable task amongst other key members of the organising committee, such as the sector marshals.

Members of the public who are definitely known to be opposed to rallying ought to be avoided when a route is planned in the first place. But those who are slightly against the idea of rally cars passing by their property in the middle of the night must be pacified in advance, and a ' Quiet Zone ' set-up for all competitors on the stretch of road, or through the village affected.

Wherever a Clerk of the Course might think it would be rather fun for his rally to use private roads, permission must be sought from the landowner. It is the PR's job to ensure that the owner is kept happy. County Councils will have to be visited whenever a bridle path is required for use on a rally route.

The PR work should not be done too far ahead of an event, otherwise the act of informing the public will be largely wasted. But visiting all the people involved may take quite a long time, so a compromise has to be reached so that there is at least sufficient time available prior to the event for all the visitations to be made comfortably. If any route changes become necessary as a result of PR, then these must be carefully recorded. He will in turn pass these to the Clerk of the Course, who is then expected to inform the RAC for them to check out the changes on their master record of the particular map.

The most important places, where PR is vital, are of course where competitors are likely to be trying the hardest, such as on the selectives, which will be on public roads albeit, it is hoped, sparsely inhabited. And because of the increasing motorised mobility of the public, as well as the apparent growth in mass popularity of the sport, more and more rallies seem to be attracting more and more spectators, it is a wise organiser who lays on special spectating places where this public can be controlled. Such places should be chosen so that the access and departure of spectators' cars using other roads does not prove to be a problem to those used by the very competing cars that they have come to watch. The most consciencious PR will compile a list of the most suitable vantage points where interested spectators can watch the passing of the rally. Such a list should ideally have the directions of approach and departure given for each point, so that the public can stay out of the way of the action. To complete the package deal for spectators a list of competitors and their numbers can be included. It might help even further, if the PR hands out an entry and spectator-point list to any pro-rally members of the public he may discover on his tour of visiting the people, to let them know all about the event.

If the event has sponsors, this PR package can well be presented by them at their expense, to further the overall value they can gain from sponsoring the event.

Glossary

Afon: River in Welsh

All-nighter: All night event, usually from around 2200 hours, through until 0600 hours or so the following morning.

Appendix J: Appendix (or one section of the FIA's rules governing vehicle modifications permitted for various forms of conventional motor sport) usually referred to in many events' regulations, with which competitors must ensure their cars comply. This applies particularly for Internationals.

ASR: Additional supplementary regulations, extra to the standard master regulations suggested by the RAC for organising motor clubs. These can be posted to competitors either in a particular event's regulations, or with the final instructions, once a competitor's entry has been accepted.

Average: Average speed of an event or section. So a ' 30 average ' would be a part of a rally that competitors would be expected to cover by the organisers at a 30 mph average—if they are to remain on time and penalty free. British road events are supposed, according to RAC rules, to be run at an absolute maximum of 30 mph.

Bag tank: Bag petrol tank, used widely in racing cars to reduce fire risk through there being the absolute minimum of air with the petrol in the tank.

Baulk: Very unpopular with top drivers, novices are usually guilty of baulking faster cars by not moving out of their way and allowing them through. If a car catches up another car on a rally, it is quicker and should be let through. Scandinavians will not tolerate baulking. They simply move any baulkers

smartly out of the way with their front end. This usually cures
the offender of the habit.

BCF: Chemical used in some fire extinguishers to put out a fire
by cutting off all oxygen from the flames. BCF does not make a
mess on mechanical components like a foam or powder filled
extinguisher does.

Bell: Make of crash helmet, perhaps the first with chin protection integrally built across the front of the helmet. More
suitable for racing as conversation with such a helmet is rather
difficult.

Bend reading: Activity of navigators reading the corners off the
map to their drivers. On OS one inch to the mile maps, every
twist and turn (or almost every!) of even the most minor by-
way are discernible with the help of a map magnifier.

Biode: Cibie's performance headlight unit, ideal for rallyists
as two separate reflectors are incorporated within the same
unit, both using powerful quartz-iodine bulbs.

Black Spot: Area which the RAC have decreed *Black* for the
passage of registered events, due to a previous complaint.
Organisers are expected to enforce a penalty of exclusion if
any competitor is found to have entered or traversed a square
on the map, which has been *Blacked,* and about which competitors have been forewarned in the final instructions by the
organisers.

Blackwell: Name of a manufacturer of average-speed rotating
disc-type computers, used more generally on rallies when
average speeds were varied throughout the event, and so
timing. Therefore the average speed being achieved was likely
to be marked on sight by each marshal. A Blackwell could be
used for all sorts of in-car calculations of estimated fuel consumption, estimated time of arrival at a certain average speed,
as well as, by feeding in distance covered and time spent covering that distance, what average was being achieved at any time
during an event.

Blue Book: Annual publication from the RAC's Motor Sport
Division, in which all the rules, governing the sport, com-
petitors as well as organisers, are laid out in their latest form.
Every competitor must have a ' Blue Book ' as a first step to-

wards knowing the rules. A copy is supplied to every RAC Competition Licence holder.

Bonus: Payment paid by vehicle and component manufacturers on international events to successful product users for overall, team and class wins. Bonus awards can often amount to considerably more than prize money, albeit never very much in rallying.

BTRDA: British Trials and Rally Drivers' Association.

Calling up: Habit of co-drivers and navigators calling up the time that they would really like to be clocked by a marshal—rather than the one that is in actual fact upon that marshal's clock. Calling up will always occur if a crew is late.

Chisel: Form of long stud used in Scandinavia to cut into packed ice and snow. Chisels do not last very long on thin icy patches or tarmac, unlike studs, which in certain countries are fitted to tyres all the year round.

The Circuit: Circuit of Ireland.

Clean: Meaning covering any section or even, in exceptional circumstances, a complete rally route, without losing any time at all. If a section is said to be *Cleanable,* it means it is possible to cover it without loss of time. A *Clean Sheet* means that a crew has covered the rally to that point, without a single penalty point.

Clerk of the Course: Leader of any organising team responsible in the final analysis for every facet of the event, although with specific responsibility for the course itself, its suitability, and opening and closing it.

Closing date: Date by when all entries have to be received by the Secretary of the event.

Closed event: Only open to members of the organising club to enter.

Closed road: Road closed to other members of the public, with one-way rally traffic using it only, usually employed in countries where this is allowed for Special Stages.

Co-driver: Navigator on the longer events, such as would be the case with International status rallies. In charge of the office aspects of the car, the navigation, as well as deputising for the driver, whenever the number one wants some sleep.

Control: Officially designated control point.

Control area: Area set aside by the organisers as being within each control. Often it is not allowed for competitors to hang back within the control area from booking in at the clock, nor to work on their cars.

Co-promoted: Event, the organisation of which has become a joint effort between one or more clubs, whose entry list can be open to members of those organising clubs, as well as those from any of the clubs on the invited list if the event was a Restricted one.

Coupe: An award on many of the classic events in the unlikely event of any competitor covering the whole route without loss of time. The most famous *Coupe* of all is a *Coupe de Alpes* on the Alpine Rally.

Cumulative mileage: Mileage in a road book from the start of the event, or from the last major control, up to a particular instruction, as opposed to the distance from the last instruction.

Cut: When a competitor has to miss out a control point due to becoming late on the overall time, needing as much time as possible to reach the final control within the permitted lateness.

Dead time: Often time spent traversing parts of the route declared by organisers as neutral because of unfriendly natives, or the need for competitors to be quiet when going through a village, is termed as *Dead,* or free from timing.

Decibel meter: Device used by organisers to measure the noise output of competitors' exhausts, both at the start and on the route itself.

Direction of approach: Each control normally has a specified direction of approach with which it is obligatory for all competitors to comply.

Doughnut: Transmission coupling linking driveshaft to differential output spider.

Driving test: Can be introduced on an event, either as a test on its own or merely as a tie-decider, consisting of cars having to follow a predetermined set route in, out, and around a collection of oil drums and straw bales, entering ' boxes ' (imaginary garages), and stopping across lines—to time.

Drop: Lose units of time, usually minutes on road sections.

DS 11: Ferodo competition specification brake pad material, virtually standard equipment on British rally cars' disc brakes.

Eight figure reference: Absolute pinpoint in map references, normally six figure, in this case another division further on each of the three figure parts of the reference, really only used where there is a maze of minor tracks, and accuracy of direction of approach and/or departure to that control is absolutely crucial.

Eolite: Illuminated map magnifier used by most of the top navigators.

Épreuve: Specially timed section on a European event, on the lines of our own special stages, which are often called *Épreuves* by some organisers as an attempt at international terminology.

Étage: More recent term for *Épreuve*, directly similar to our own special stage, or can mean a complete part of an event.

FIA: Federation Internationale de L'Automobile, the governing body of conventional motor sport, under whose auspices the RAC Motor Sport Division operate in Great Britain.

Final instructions: Paperwork despatched to each competitor by the organisers by which he can be informed of his starting number, the time he has to report at the start, a list of out-of-bounds areas, as well as any advanced route information that might be helpful for him to put on his maps, before he reports to the start.

Flexilight: Type of flexible map reading light made by Butlers.

Flying finish: The end of a special stage can be a flying one, in that competitors are timed as they flash across a finish line prior to their coming to a halt a little further along the route to collect a time card, or have their road book duly filled in. In such cases, the time keeper beside the flying finish line will be in touch with the marshal at the halt line by a telephone link.

Force Majeure: Where a decision of *Force Majeure* is awarded to a particular query/complaint/protest situation, this means that, whatever the individual misfortune or localised hazard encountered unfairly by a competitor, the luck of the draw is the order of the day. *Force Majeure* can therefore mean bad luck, or good fortune, all according to how specific circumstances affect the results of the individuals concerned.

Full harness: Safety belts incorporating two shoulder straps, as well as a lap one.

Gemini: Make of navigator's trip measuring device, either single or double odometers, fitted with turn off, plus and minus controls for when the trip figures need to be stopped, added to or, in the event of a navigational error and a subsequent retracing of steps, reduced.

General classification: Final finishing order, after the protest period has elapsed, determining the overall placings, regardless of class.

Goer: Used to describe whether a road/track is passable or not. Actual weather conditions can, of course, affect the viability of a *goer,* thus making it a *non-goer.*

Grass triangle: Describing a grass island in the middle of a junction or fork, directions of approach may have to be very carefully observed on such occasions.

Graviner: Fire system, automatically set off by inertia, temperature or manual controls, in the cockpit or outside, used primarily in out-and-out racing car applications.

Green Card: Necessary international insurance documentation for the competitor rallying abroad.

Grey Spot: Specific places known by the Rally Authorisation Department at the RAC Motor Sport Division to be anti-rally or unsuitable for the passage of an event, although no actual complaints have been received or incidents on rallies have occurred on these parts of the map. Organisers' submitted routes are carefully modified to avoid the traversing of *Grey Spots.*

Group 1: FIA classification for standard motor vehicles taking part in sporting events. Cars in this group must only use standard components with a minimum of 5,000 identical basic models having been manufactured.

Group 2: A further FIA classification for special touring cars, with catalogued and approved modifications permitted, as well as any modifications to the original parts, with a minimum of 1,000 identical models having been manufactured.

Group 3: A further FIA classification for series production grand touring cars, again with the proviso that 1,000 identical models have been manufactured.

Group 4: Another FIA classification for special grand touring cars, of which 500 similar models would have to have been made.

Group 6: The FIA sub-division for one-offs, regarded as experimental prototypes. Not many top rallies cater for cars of this group, although on club events, modifications can usually be limitless.

Halda: Manufacturers of average speed and trip measuring equipment. The Halda twin tripmeter is virtually standard equipment on any well prepared British rally car.

Half-inch: OS maps with half-inch to one mile scale, rarely used on the mass of British club events, apart from overall route and service planning.

Half-nighter: Event, the overall time schedule of which only takes half a night, usually starting at 2200 hours and finishing at 0200 hours.

Handbrake turn: Method by which really sharp bends or hairpin junctions can be negotiated with the minimum of time wastage at one bite, simply by the driver holding on the handbrake, smartly locking up his car's rear wheels, whilst approaching a corner at speed, turning the steering wheel, so that the tail spins round and the vehicle changes direction within its own length.

Homologation Form: A necessary document for the international competitor to produce at scrutineering for his particular make and type of car to be checked for eligibility against the details included on such a form. These FIA forms are available at a fee from the RAC Motor Sport Division.

They include permissible modifications that can be carried out by a particular type of vehicle's owner within the various groupings.

Ice Note: Method by which a co-driver can mark up his pace notes the last minute before he has to direct his driver over each particular stage to include the very latest ice, patchy ice, snow and patchy snow conditions. On winter rallies, accurate *Ice Notes* are vital, so that the right type of tyre can be selected and the driver can be warned of any sudden ice that could catch him unawares.

Iodine: Form of high performance headlamp and auxiliary light bulb.

Indemnification: Usually required to be signed by all crewmembers before they set off on an event, so that the organising club and its officials are absolved from any potential claim that might arise in the unfortunate event of an accident.

In-line fuse: Simplest type of fuse, not requiring a permanent fuse board, simply fitted into each auxilliary feed. Of particular value for the runs out to the extra lights at the front.

Intercom: Battery operated system by which, in the modern noisy rally car, the co-driver can make his instructions heard by his driver. This is absolutely vital, where helmets are being worn, as is the case on the more important events.

Invited clubs: Restricted events in Great Britain will be open to entries from members of the organising club, as well as members of those clubs on the event's Invited list.

IRDC: International Rally Drivers' Club.

Judge of fact: Most organisers will decide that wherever there is a confliction of opinion between marshal and competitor, over whether that competitor did or did not comply with some point of the regulations, then the official involved would be said to be *Judge of fact,* therefore being given the last say.

Kilometre: ⅝ of a GB mile.
Kilometre square: Squares on OS one mile to the inch maps.
K's: Kilometres.

Lap and diagonal: Safety belt, consisting of a lap strap, one half of which loops via the lap buckle to form the one diagonal strap as well. This type of belt is the easiest of all to wear, especially if a navigator has much gate opening to do.

Lap strap: Safety belt retaining the wearer in his place purely by a lap strap.

Leaf Spring: Form of suspension spring using lengths of spring steel, or leaves, to make up the spring, the leaves being clasped together by shackles.

Left-foot braking: Technique used by the Scandinavians firstly, now used by many leading rally drivers, particularly on front-wheel drive cars, whereby the left foot is used to apply the brakes against the effects of acceleration to avoid the drive wheels locking up. This technique is of great value on loose or icy surfaces to reduce a vehicle's speed as safely and as quickly as possible. The car can also be set up at the very last minute using this skill.

Lever-arm dampers: Shock absorbers that use a lever arm method of operation, as opposed to a telescopic unit.

Limited slip: Limited slip differentials are those, which limit the spin of the drive wheel with the lightest load over it, as would be the case for an inside drive wheel, whether front- or rear-wheel drive, during cornering. Their advantage on loose surface work and in inclement weather is all too obvious.

Map magnifier: Illuminated gadget, by which the navigator's map can be seen by him more easily, with less driver distraction than with a map light.

Marked map: A navigator's map marked up with all relevant tips and local knowledge, likely to be useful on an event. This can either be a navigator's personal map, the information progressively added over many rallies, or can be one marked up with control points or their intended route by an organiser.

Marking up a map: Activity carried out over many long evenings by all navigators worth their salt. As maps become tatty, so the information ought to be transferred onto a new one. It is wise because of fire, floods, mud, or the wind carrying away a navigator's most valuable map, for a master set of marked maps to be kept by the navigator safely at home.

Minilite: Most popular of lightweight (but immensely strong) magnesium alloy road wheels, used by most of the factory teams.

Monza cap: Flip-up petrol tank filler cap, ideal as the cap is hinged, affixed to the tank neck, and so unlikely to become dislodged, or left behind in some confused petrol station attendant's pocket.

Navigational event: Event, in which the navigation plays the most important part in the determination of that event's results, as opposed to team, individual driver or car performance.

Navigational notes: Used on major internationals by co-drivers to acurately follow, with a minimum of looking at maps or organisers' paperwork, the intended route between special sections, which would then be charted in more detail by a set of pace notes. Such notes would include mileages, road numbers and fuel facilities.

Neutral section: That part of any route which is untimed, specifically so that competitors are not encouraged to cause inconvenience to local inhabitants and road users by their having to hurry to be on time.

Night halt: Official rest halt in the middle of an event, so that drivers can snatch food and sleep, or effect a swap with their co-driver.

Noise Control: A control specially laid on for the purpose of checking, and penalising if necessary, competitors whose exhaust noise exceeds the laid down minimum.

Nomex: Flame-proof material used in the manufacture of competition clothing and overalls.

Non-goer: A track which is deemed to be (often by experience!) impassable even for the purposes of the most intrepid rallyist.

Nyloc: Type of locking nut.

On: Section of route that can be completed in the time allowed.
One-inch: Ordnance Survey map, one inch to one mile scale.

One minuter: Section for which a time allowed of one minute has been set by the organisers for the competitors. At a maximum permitted average of 30 mph on public roads, open to other road users, this means a distance between controls of half a mile.

OS: Ordnance Survey maps.

Oscar: Perhaps the most popular auxiliary lamp of all, made by Cibie.

Out-of-bounds: Area deemed to be out of bounds for competitors, usually enforceable on pain of exclusion.

Pace note: System by which international co-drivers read every twist and turn of the special sections to their drivers. The route, being announced in advance by the organisers, will be covered for the compilation of such notes during a recce.

Padding: Parts of a rally that do nothing further than link the interesting and challenging parts.

Parc Fermé: Park for rally cars, in which no work is permitted at all, or at very least only by the actual crew members, during an event at night or rest halts.

Passage check: Control point, manned by marshals, but untimed, the passage of competitors being recorded only—regardless of how late (or early!) they are.

Plot: Business of plotting map references.

Plot and Bash: An event or section where competitors are only handed out the map references, determining the intended route, precisely at their start time.

Pop-in: Ice studs are fired into, pre-prepared at manufacture, holes in tread blocks.

Powrlok: Salisbury's limited slip differential.

PR: Public Relations.

Prime: 'Ye Olde' word, very fashionable on Lieges, and indeed on the World Cup London to Mexico, for the special stages, though not necessarily on closed public roads it must be stated.

Printing clock: Time clock at a control, where competitors record the time for themselves, like a clock-in at a factory. Legibility of the printed time on any card must be carefully checked by any co-driver before a driver is allowed to roar on to the next control.

Protest: After provisional results have been announced, but before the protest period is up, any disagreements with the results team's findings can be disputed democratically by any competitor with a protest, necessarily accompanied with a fee.

Protex: Form of fire resistant material used by some manufacturers of racing clothing, being worn by increasing numbers of present-day rallyists. Cheaper than Nomex.

Prune: Method by which an organiser can tighten up an ' on paper ' route, approved by the RAC's Motor Sport Division as being within the maximum overall permitted average speed requirements, and in reality cause competitors to exceed this average—if they are not too late that is!

QI: Quartz-iodine lighting, usually referring to the bulbs.

Quarter-inch: Ordnance Survey maps, quarter-inch to each mile scale.

Quiet Zone: Area decreed by the organisers, through which competitors must keep their noise right down. Often such areas will be marshalled by noise marshals, equipped with a decibel meter, as well as being judges of fact that competitors have dipped their lights and are driving sensibly.

Reading the road: Activity of the navigator reading the nature of the road from the map, out aloud to the driver.

Recce: Reconnaissance trip by one or both crew members over the rally route, where route information has been released in advance by the organisers, with resultant compilation of navigation and pace notes.

Regularity: Events where checks on the average speed of competitors against the average set by the organisers are made at disclosed or undisclosed points along the route. The marking on ' Regularity ' events is all done on adherence to the average set, as opposed to straight-forward time loss.

Regulations: Organisers are required to publish and distribute the rules and details of their event for prospective entrants to see what the event is all about.

Restart: After a neutralisation, rest or night halt, there will be a restart of proceedings and timing. On such occasions it is usual for the gaps in the entry, through various retirements, to be taken out, so that the rally convoy is as condensed as possible for ease of administration and to avoid an excess of straggling over several hours.

Restricted: Event of restricted status, where entries are restricted to members of invited clubs only.

Road book: Route information on an event, whether by 'Tulip' diagrams, or just a list of map references with approach, departure, distance between, and time allowed between such points, in book form. On smaller events, the 'Road Book' can be of course just a run-off circular type affair or a single sheet of paper even. A precious item as many a top crew has been put out of an event before now by its loss.

Romer: Portable scale gadget, by which a navigator can plot map references with the utmost accuracy. A romer should always have a string threaded through it, so that it can be safely carried around a navigator's neck to avoid it being lost at some crucial moment, perhaps after he has had to leap out to check in at a control point or open a gate.

Roof light: Long-range swivel driving lamp, controlled by the co-driver or navigator from within the cockpit. Now illegal in many countries.

Rough: Term for any piece of rough track or surface.

Route card: Abbreviated road book, with all the route information upon it.

Scrubbing: Removal of certain sections of the route from the results of an event afterwards, as a result of something going wrong with the timing or organisation.

Sealed watch: Timing on some rallies is carried out by this system, where a competitor's own watch, or one provided for each competitor, is set to either master rally time or to an individual time per competitor. The watch is then sealed into a clear fronted container.

Secret Check: Organisers can set up such checks to observe competitors' driving standards and/or average speeds to ensure that these do not exceed their laid down maxi-

N

mums, particularly on easy link sections on main roads.

Secretary of the Meeting: Responsible for all the paperwork on the organisers' side of an event.

Sector Marshal: Chief marshal of a sector, under the overall control of the chief marshal, with specific responsibility for looking after a group of controls or stages.

Seeding: Method by which the exact starting order on a rally is determined on past performances plus present form, always bound to be unpopular with one section or the other of any entry. Skilful seeding is vital to avoid the quicker crews being plagued by baulking.

Selective: Specially timed part of a road section, usually to the nearest second as opposed to the nearest minute. Selectives are often fairly long and are on roads open to other road users, as opposed to out-and-out special stages.

Service: Outside assistance, on an organised basis, to keep a rally car maintained and repaired as necessary whilst a rally is in progress.

Seven day clock: Dashboard clock for total time elapsed purposes, usually ex-Services.

Six figure reference: Conventional map reference to a further tenth each way from the ' along the corridor—up the stairs ' basic decision to a particular kilometre square.

Skid Plate: Tabs of steel sheet welded onto any protruding edge under a rally car, so that there is then less chance of any rock or protrusion causing damage to the underside's vital components.

Slot: Road or track off the one already being used.

Special Stage: Piece of road or track closed to other road users, with one-way special stage competitor traffic only, with target times set at much higher average speeds than the road section, or even the selectives if any.

Starting order: Order of starting determined by the organisers' seeding. This can be varied during an event for a restart after a halt according to general classification at that point.

Straight-cut: Usually referring to gear teeth that are straight-cut for greater strength, as opposed to helical, all at the expense of increased noise though.

Straight line: Type of navigation, used by some ' navigational ' event organisers, comprising of a straight line system to signify the route that competitors should follow, with all the various turnings off on either side of the real road shown as branches off the straight line.

Strut: Suspension leg, such as the Macpherson strut that it so widely used on so many Ford models.

Spats: Attachments so that an increased tread area is covered where this spreads outside the bodyline, in the form of screwed or riveted-on eyebrows or complete welded-in wider wheel-arches.

Sumpguard: Guard to protect the underside of an engine and also the transmission, where this is an integral part or near to it, fabricated out of steel or cast magnesium alloy.

' Targa' timing: Method of timing introduced to club events on the Oxford University Drivers' Club's Targa Rusticana, by which every car, if it is on time at each control, is due to arrive at every timed point at the same time on the clocks—the watches being offset from one control to the next by the number of minutes allowed for each section of the route. Much the easiest method to employ for organiser and competitor alike.

Target Time: Time allowed for the competitor to complete the section.

Ten tenths: Flat out, maximum effort.

Tenths: Tenths of miles on OS one inch to one mile maps.

Tie Decider: Section of a rally, the timing of which is used by the organisers as a decider of ties, often carried out to the nearest second where the rest of the route is timed to the nearest whole minute.

Tight: Difficult to cover the particular section in the time allowed, timing being ' tight '.

Time card: Each timed or special section finish control can hand out its own time card to each competitor as his proof of visiting that particular control point. Such cards are marked up and signed by each marshal in charge of each point, whilst the actual time of arrival, or time achieved over the stage, is added onto each card.

Time clocks: This can either be merely a clock which the marshal looks at to record the time of a competitor's arrival, or it can be a clock which requires a time card to be inserted into it for a print-out to be made. Clocking a time in this way can either be carried out by the marshal or the competitor, according to the system employed by the particular organiser.

Time elapsed: Time that cannot be regained by setting off from an official halt early, as it has been clocked up even in the form of penalty.

Timing: Covering the overall timing of any event, the method of penalising competitors by their being late anywhere along the route.

Timing on sight: Method by which competitors are timed by marshals ' on sight ' rather than when they actually pull up alongside the marshals' car or control table.

Timekeeper: Officially appointed by the organisers as a timekeeper. He should preferably be an RAC officially registered timekeeper, as listed in the ' Blue Book ', particularly if the timing is for a circuit special stage.

Toe-heel: Driving so that the toes operate the brake pedal, whilst the heel on the same foot operates the throttle pedal, or vice versa, so that the engine speed can be adjusted and a lower gear engaged whilst braking is being carried out.

Total Regularity: Event where the average speed set by the organisers is likely to be checked at any time along the route.

Three-ply: Badly breaking up surface, though still metalled.

Thrash: Arduous event.

Tripmeter: Mechanical device, usually positioned on the passenger side of the cockpit for measuring distances between junctions as accurately as possible. One or two meters can be used, together with plus and minus for adjustment to totals. Tripmeters can be obtained from Halda or Gemini, in miles or kilometres, whilst a whole range of gears are available, for adjustments to be made according to a particular vehicle's gearing and wheel and tyre sizes.

Tulip diagrams: System of road book marking for navigational instructions to appear diagramatically with ' Tulip ' symbols. This method was used originally on the Tulip rally.

Turret: Area on a bodyshell around a top suspension mounting in the shape of a turret. Often vehicles, such as the Ford Escort, with slanting rear shock absorbers, can be modified to great effect by the fitting of a pair of turrets in the boot, so that vertical dampers can be used, thus resulting in better axle location.

Tweak: Modify, or tune.

Twelve car event: Closed to one club events, extra the road licensing rules laid out, in accordance with the MOT's wishes, by the RAC Motor Sport Division, limited to a maximum of twelve starters.

Twinmaster: Two tripmeters in the one unit, so that total mileage, as well as mileage between each route instruction in a road book, can be followed. Twinmaster is the unit manufactured by Halda, the Taximeter people, leaders in this field.

Undershield: Sheet of hard material, either steel or dural, to protect part or all of the underside of a vehicle for rough road work.

VG 95: Specification label for anti-fade brake lining material made by Ferodo, widely used on rally cars, all round on an all-drum brake layout, or in combination with *DS 11* disc brake pads on a disc/drum set-up.

WDA: Wrong direction of approach, to a control. Often penalised as heavily as missing a control altogether.

White: As on OS maps, but usually by rallyists to describe any minor road or track that might be considered to be interesting on an event.

Wishbone: Two pronged, wishbone-shaped major suspension part, fitted top or bottom.

Works: Factory prepared.

Year bar: Collected annually on some of the more important events, different colours according to finisher, non-finisher, or official even.

Yellow: Colour of road on OS map, graded between white, and brown and red.

Yump: Auto-flying, can be to yump—the activity; or a yump—the hazard responsible.

APPENDIX

Useful Addresses

Air horns Bosch Ltd, Rhodes Way, Radlett Road, Watford, Hertfordshire (Watford 44233)
Fiamm (and others), Harry Moss Ltd, 424 Kingston Road, London SW 20 (01–540–8131)

Brakes Automotive Products (Lockheed, and Borg and Beck clutches) Competition Dept, Tachbrook Road, Leamington Spa, Warwickshire (0926–27000)
Girling Ltd, Kings Road, Tyseley, Birmingham (021–706–3371)
Brake linings Don, Small and Parkes Ltd, Hendham Vale, Manchester (061–205–2371)
Ferodo Competitions Dept, Chapel-en-le-Frith, near Stockport, Cheshire (0298–81–2520)

Competition departments Ford Motor Co Ltd, Competitions, Boreham Airfield, Boreham, nr Chelmsford, Essex (0245–28–661)
Official customer tuning and performance parts divisions of manufacturers
British Leyland Special Tuning Department, MG Factory, Abingdon-on-Thames, Berkshire (Abingdon 251)
Chrysler UK Customer Tuning Department, Gate 5, Humber Works, Humber Road, Stoke, Coventry, Warwickshire (0203–52144)
Ford Advanced Vehicle Operation (AVO), Arisdale Avenue, South Ockendon, Essex (South Ockendon 3434)

Electrical preparation Joseph Lucas Racing Department, Joseph Lucas Electrical, Great King Street, Birmingham (021–554–5252), and thence at local Sales and Service Depots

Fire extinguishers Bradville Ltd, Bradex Works, Huddersfield Road, Wyke, Bradford, Yorks (0274–676272)
Firemaster Extinguishing Ltd, Firex Works, Friendly Place, Lewisham Road, London SE 13 (01–692–6231)
Plus Gas Co Ltd, Stirling Road, Acton, London W3 (01–992–0093/7)
Simoniz Ltd, 125 High Holborn, London WC1 (01–242–4384)

Heated and laminated screens Triplex Safety Glass Co Ltd, 1 Albemarle Street, London W1 (01–493–8171)
Wallace Windscreens, 98 Webber Street, London SE1 (01–928–5228)

Helmets Checkpoint Race and Rally Equipment Ltd, 83 Euston Road, London NW1 (01–387–0601)
Formula One, 21 Ganton Street, Carnaby Street, London W1 (01–437–3968)
Les Leston Racekit, 315 Finchley Road, London NW3 (01–435–2221)
Jaycessories Ltd, Highbury Road, Peterborough (Peterborough 68247/8)
Marble Arch Racing and Rally Division, 314 High Holborn, London WC1 (01–242–8655)
Road and Racing Accessories (Holborn) Ltd, 8 Proctor Street, London WC1 (01–242–3080)

Gordon Spice Group, City Speed Shop, 76 Bishopsgate, London EC2 (01–588–3881)

J and J Stanton Ltd, 782 Harrow Road, Sudbury, Middlesex (01–908–2800)

Instruments Smiths Industries (Motor Accessory Division), Cricklewood Works, Cricklewood, London NW2 (01–452–3333)

Yazaki, Time Instrument Manufacturers Ltd, 928 High Road, Finchley, London N12 (01–445–0491)

Lamps Bosch Ltd, 166 Radlett Road, Watford, Hertfordshire (Watford 44233)

Carello, Lyall Lusted Ltd, Vincent Works, Vincent Lane, Dorking, Surrey (0306–4091/2)

Cibie, Britover (Continental) Ltd, 387-389 Chapter Road, London NW2 (01–459–7256)

Hella, Hanworth Lane, Chertsey, Surrey (Chertsey 2291)

Joseph Lucas Sales and Service, Great Hampton Street, Birmingham 18 (021–236–5050)

Lumax, Ceag Ltd, Queen's Road, Barnsley, Yorkshire (0226–6842)

Marchal Distributors Ltd, Great West Road, Brentford, Middlesex (01–560–2111)

Wipac Group Ltd, London Road, Buckingham (0280–2–3031)

Lamp brackets Roland Kerr Ltd, 125 Tarring Road, Worthing, Sussex (0903–7878)

Joseph Lucas Sales and Service, Great Hampton Street, Birmingham 18 (021–236–5050)

Super Sport, 11 Colville Road, South Acton Industrial Estate, Acton, London W3 (01–993–1122)

Map reading lights Butlers Ltd, Grange Road, Small Heath, Birmingham 10 (021–772–4393)

Mudflaps Tudor Accessories Ltd, Llanvanor Road, Childs Hill, London NW2 (01–458–1181)

Oil radiators Coventry Radiator and Presswork Co Ltd, Canley, Coventry (Coventry 75544)

Mocal, Think Automotive Ltd, 1a Greenford Avenue, Southall, Middlesex (01–574–4652)

Serck Services, 456 Stratford Road, Sparkhill, Birmingham 11 (021–772–5865)

Overalls Basically the same suppliers and stockists as helmets

Performance parts Allard Motor Co Ltd, 51 Upper Richmond Road, Putney, London SW15 (01–874–2333)

Arden Conversions Ltd, Penn Lane, Tanworth-in-Arden, Solihull, Warwickshire (0564–7–3368)

Blydenstein, 4 Station Works, Shepreth, near Royston, Hertfordshire (Melbourn 1251/2)

British Vita Racing Team, Smithy Bridge, Fletchers Road, Littleborough, Lancs (0706–78972)

Broadspeed Ltd, Banbury Road, Southam, Leamington Spa, Warwickshire (0926–81–3191)

Emery, Aspenlea Road, London W6 (01–385–8584)

Hartwell, 43 Holdenhurst Road, Bournemouth, Hampshire (0202–26566)

Janspeed, Southampton Road, Salisbury, Wiltshire (0722–22082)

Oselli, Industrial Estate, Stanton Harcourt Road, Eynsham, Oxford (Evenlode 522/545)

Raceproved, 177 Uxbridge Road, Hanwell, London W7 (01–579–0991)

Superspeed, 482 Ley Street, Ilford, Essex (01–554–8307)

Super Sport, 11 Colville Road, South Acton Industrial Estate, Acton, London W3 (01–993–1122)

Ian Walker Racing, 236 Woodhouse Road, London N12 (01–368–6281/3)

John Willment (Mitcham) Ltd, 189-191 Streatham Road, Mitcham, Surrey (01–648–0071)

Withers of Winsford, Smokehall Lane, Wharton, Winsford, Cheshire (Winsford 4422)

David Wood Engineering, Chiswick Avenue, Mildenhall Industrial Estate, Mildenhall, Suffolk (Mildenhall 7124)

Preparation Clarke and Simpson, Sloane Square, London SW1 (01–730–0436)

Coburn Improvements, Netherhall Gardens, London NW3 (01–435–6743)

Will Sparrow Rally Preparation, 2 Redditch Road, Studley, Worcs (07395–3212)

Super Sport, 11 Colville Road, South Acton Industrial Estate, Acton, London W3 (01–993–1122)

Ian Walker Racing, 236 Woodhouse Road, London N12 (01–368–6281/3)

David Wood Engineering, Chiswick Avenue, Mildenhall Industrial Estate, Mildenhall, Suffolk (Mildenhall 7124)

Administration and licences RAC Motor Sport Division, 31 Belgrave Square, London SW1 (01–235–8601)

Rally accessories Alexander Engineering, Thame Road, Haddenham, Aylesbury, Buckinghamshire (0844–29–345)

Checkpoint Race and Rally Equipment Ltd, 83 Euston Road, London NW1 (01–387–0601)

Jaycessories Ltd, Highbury Street, Peterborough (Peterborough 68247/8)

J. and J. Stanton Ltd, 782 Harrow Road, Sudbury, Middlesex (01–908–2800)

Withers of Winsford, Smokehall Lane, Wharton, Winsford, Cheshire (Winsford 4422)

Roll-over bars John Aley Racing Ltd, Church Lane, Whittlesford, Cambridge (Sawston 3293)

Bijo Ltd, Rossway Farm, Little Bushey Lane, Bushey, Herts (01–950–5477)

Ron Haynes Motor Sports Ltd, Cardain House, Burkes Road, Beaconsfield New Town, Beaconsfield, Bucks (Beaconsfield 5620)

Safety belts Britax Ltd, Proctor Works, Chertsey Road, Byfleet, Surrey (Byfleet 41121)

Kangol Magnet Ltd, 39 Fitzroy Square,

London W1 (01–636–8468)

Willans, Stockbridge Racing, Grosvenor Garage, Stockbridge, Hants (Stockbridge 711)

Screenwashers Trico-Folberth Ltd, Great West Road, Brentford, Middlesex (01–560–2111)

Tudor Accessories Ltd, Llanvanor Road, Childs Hill, London NW2 (01–458–1181)

Seats Corbeau Equipe Ltd, 76 Mount Pleasant, Hastings (Hastings 6360)

Restall Brothers Ltd, Floodgate Street, Birmingham 5 (021–772–4937)

Shock absorbers Armstrong Patents Co Ltd, Eastgate, Beverley, Yorkshire (0482–882212)

Bilstein, 5828 Ennepetal-Altenvoerde, Postfach 15, West Germany (02333–20–22)

Girling Ltd, Kings Road, Tyseley, Birmingham (021–706–3371)

Koni, J. W. E. Banks and Sons Ltd, Crowland, Peterborough (0724–81)

Spax Ltd, 61 Forbes Road, London NW5 (01–485–6721)

Woodhead, Kingsway, Ossett, Yorks (09–243–3521/9)

Spark plugs Autolite Motor Products Ltd, Wharf Road, Ponders End, Enfield, Middlesex (01–804–1221)

Bosch Ltd, Radlett Road, Watford, Hertfordshire (Watford 44233)

Champion Sparking Plug Co Ltd, Feltham, Middlesex (01–759–6442)

Steering wheels Astrali Accessories (Midlands) Ltd, Anglian Road, Redhouse Industrial Estate, Aldridge, Staffordshire (0922–53501)

Formula Steering Wheels Ltd, Bank Street, Gravesend, Kent (0474–64814)

Intertech Developments Ltd, 78–80 High Street, Earls Colne, Essex (0787–5–790)

Peco, Sandford Street, Birkenhead, Cheshire (051–647–6041)

Sumpguards British Leyland Special Tuning Department, MG Factory,

Abingdon-on-Thames, Berkshire (Abingdon 251)

Ford AVO, Arisdale Avenue, South Ockendon, Essex (South Ockendon 3434)

Super Sport, 11 Colville Road, South Acton Industrial Estate, Acton, London W3 (01–993–1122)

Tech Del Ltd, 32–36 Telford Way, Brunel Road, Acton, London W3 (01–743–0103)

Tripmeters Gemini, G. A. Stanley Palmer Ltd, Elmbridge Works, Island Farm Avenue, West Molesley Trading Estate, East Molesey, Surrey (01–979–7254)

Halda Ltd, 3 Brandon Road, York Way, London N7 (01–607–1207)

Tyres Dunlop Co Ltd, Competitions Department, Fort Dunlop, Birmingham 24 (021–373–2121)

Firestone Tyre and Rubber Co Ltd, Great West Road, Brentford, Middlesex (01–560–4141)

Goodyear Tyre and Rubber Co Ltd, Competitions Department, Bushbury, Wolverhampton, Staffs (0902–22321)

Michelin Tyre Co Ltd, 160 Brompton Road, London SW3 (01–589–1460)

Pirelli Ltd, 343 Euston Road, London NW1 (01–387–3131)

Semperit Tyres, Wexham Road, Slough, Buckinghamshire (Slough 31737)

Wheels British Leyland Special Tuning Department, MG Factory, Abingdon-on-Thames, Berkshire (Abingdon 251)

Cosmic Car Accessories Ltd, Bridgeman Street, Walsall, Staffs (0922–27188/9)

Ford AVO, Arisdale Avenue, South Ockendon, Essex (South Ockendon 3434)

MAG, Mill Accessory Group Ltd, Two Counties Mill, Eaton Bray, Dunstable, Bedfordshire (0525–22–671/3)

Minilite Tech Del Ltd, 32–36 Telford Way, Brunel Road, Acton, London W3 (01–743–0103)

Wiper blades Trico-Folberth Ltd, Great West Road, Brentford, Middlesex (01–560–2111)

Index